D1257213

Reexamining Love of Wisdom

Reexamining Love of Wisdom

Philosophical Desire from Socrates to Nietzsche

JUAN CARLOS FLORES

CASCADE *Books* · Eugene, Oregon

REEXAMINING LOVE OF WISDOM
Philosophical Desire from Socrates to Nietzsche

Cascade Books
An Imprint of Wipf and Stock Publishers
199 W. 8th Ave., Suite 3
Eugene, OR 97401

www.wipfandstock.com

PAPERBACK ISBN: 978-1-4982-3762-8
HARDCOVER ISBN: 978-1-4982-3764-2
EBOOK ISBN: 978-1-4982-3763-5

Cataloguing-in-Publication data:

Names: Flores, Juan Carlos, 1970–

Title: Reexamining love of wisdom : philosophical desire from Socrates to Nietzsche / Juan Carlos Flores.

Description: Eugene, OR : Cascade Books, 2016 | Includes bibliographical references.

Identifiers: ISBN 978-1-4982-3762-8 (paperback) | ISBN 978-1-4982-3764-2 (hardcover) | ISBN 978-1-4982-3763-5 (ebook)

Subjects: LCSH: Philosophy—History. | Philosophy, European. | Philosophy and religion.

Classification: B72 .F56 2016 (paperback) | B72 .F56 (ebook)

Manufactured in the U.S.A.   09/29/16

A mi familia
Celeste
Nicolás
Alex

οὐδέν φημι ἄλλο ἐπίστασθαι ἢ τὰ ἐρωτικά.
I claim to know nothing except love.

—Socrates (Plato, *Symposium* 177E)

Contents

Acknowledgments

I am thankful to my parents for their support, to Wipf and Stock for their cooperation, and to my students throughout the years for enriching my approach to philosophy. But above all I am grateful to my family for what is best in my endeavors.

Introduction

The question, what is philosophy?—traditionally a complex question—has become an even more complex one in contemporary times. Indicating the literal meaning of the term *philosophy*, namely, love of wisdom, does not seem to help, to the extent that wisdom, like philosophy, can have a variety of meanings even among philosophers. Even elementary texts in the so-called humanities acknowledge that defining philosophy is difficult.[1] This can be surprising to those introduced to philosophy, and even rather embarrassing for philosophers, when they have trouble explaining what they do.

On the other hand, other subjects generally imply some clear conception of their basic scope and aim. Medicine, for example, studies the body in order to promote physical health. Biology studies life, economics monetary relations, and so on with the rest of the sciences: each demarks for itself an aspect of reality and endeavors to understand the properties and causes of this aspect. Similarly, the scope and aim of the different crafts and fine arts may be easily discerned. Crafts, such as agriculture and carpentry, develop various practical techniques, while fine arts, such as music and painting, engage in the various modes of creative expression. Even the rest of the so-called humanities, under which philosophy is presently classified, are unambiguous. History traces periods and events, theology studies revealed doctrine, literature the various genres of writing, etc. Naturally, within the arts and sciences there is now, more than ever, a great deal of specialization, so that members within one general field may be engaged in very different lines of work. Yet these subdivisions are easily recognizable and explained insofar as the general classifications are clearly demarked.

---

1. Cunningham and Reich, *Culture and Values*, 49.

One could say that philosophy has always delved into certain basic questions, such as questions concerning right and wrong behavior, sound reasoning, and the nature of knowledge and truth. This concern with fundamental questions, presupposed by other areas of inquiry, constitutes philosophy's identity, regardless of the vast differences among philosophical outlooks, which have varied conceptions of the very principles and possibilities of philosophy. This identity, however, is especially difficult to discern today, since now philosophy is subject to intense specialization. It has become easy for philosophers to be absorbed in their own specific lines of inquiry, and therefore more difficult for them to share and build upon common sources in their work. Naturally, those interested in the history of philosophy more easily share the resources of a tradition, but now even the history of philosophy is considered as a branch of philosophy (with its own specialized areas), as well as the province of scholars rather than philosophers in the strict sense of the word.

In part, the remote cause of this specialization is the break between philosophy and science, consummated in the seventeenth century, and the consequent specialization within modern science itself. Once the task of determining the so-called objective properties of the world was relegated to modern science, philosophy became occupied, for the most part, with issues concerning the human subject, such as the validity of scientific knowledge itself. Insofar as philosophy became philosophy of science, that is, the assessment of the implications and significance of scientific knowledge, philosophy's specialization was inevitable and proportionate to the specialization within science itself. This latching on to the various areas of human inquiry has continued to this day, where there are philosophies according to the fields to which they belong: philosophy of psychology, philosophy of biology, philosophy of literature, etc. In other words, in becoming specialized, philosophy also tended to become critical.

More generally, in the face of modern science, philosophy became focused on the problem of the nature and possibilities of human knowledge, both speculative and moral. In this new context, philosophers embraced various attitudes. For example, some still remained committed metaphysicians and sought to grasp the nature of reality, while others denied the possibility for genuine metaphysics and, therefore, saw the legitimate path of philosophy within more restrictive bounds, according to what they saw as more properly available to the mind, such as the mind's own operations. And even among those who were not metaphysicians in the strict sense of the word, divergent attitudes emerged. For phenomenologists, for example, irrespective of the intrinsic nature of things in themselves, what matters is meaning, namely, the significance of the world as it appears in human experience. Analytic philosophers, on the other hand, concentrate on the sphere that they consider as scientifically valid, namely, on language insofar as it yields sound arguments.

In other words, unlike the sciences and arts, there is divergence regarding the basic conception of the scope and aim of philosophy, in addition to the intense specialization that philosophy shares with other fields. Not surprisingly, philosophy as an academic profession is inherently specialized, since graduates concentrate on particular topics or themes and frequently continue this research throughout their careers. To conclude, against this myriad of interests, activities, and outlooks, discerning the unity among philosophers and philosophies is a hard task.

∾

The present work investigates the nature of philosophy by developing the original understanding that philosophy is a type of love, the love of wisdom. The work explains how major thinkers have embodied philosophical love in their own ways, and in doing so, it also explains how this love has undergone transformation. This transformation is quite acute, to the extent that in the modern period the core of the classical love of wisdom, common to ancient and medieval philosophy, is lost. The first two chapters develop different expressions of this classical love of wisdom, while the third chapter develops different expressions of modern philosophical desire. Accordingly, beginning with Descartes, one may speak about philosophical desire but not about love of wisdom in the classical sense. Alternatively, one may say that love of wisdom in the modern period acquires an entirely new meaning from the original, classical meaning.

However, in order to avoid confusion, this book will reserve the phrase "love of wisdom" to indicate the classical model (common to ancient and medieval philosophy), while it will indicate the love found in modern philosophies in other terms, such as philosophical desire, drive or love. These latter terms (philosophical desire, drive or love) also can be used to indicate what is common to all philosophers, whether ancient, medieval, or modern, insofar as the work of every philosopher is fueled by a certain desire, drive or love. The relative continuity of the classical model among ancient and medieval thinkers, and the modern break and adoption of new forms of philosophical desire, shall become clear in the body of this work.

As already suggested, this use of terms reflects a central thesis of this whole work. This thesis is that the classical love of wisdom, which is the basic and unifying spiritual source for ancient and medieval philosophical endeavor, is replaced eventually by the various modern impulses that define and fragment the philosophies that follow. Part of this thesis, developed throughout this work, is also showing the perennial value of the classical pursuit.

In spite of the important differences among the philosophers included here, the work does indicate a common source for all philosophy, to the extent that all philosophy is a form of human love. In tracing the transformation of philosophical love from Socrates to Nietzsche, in elaborating the continuities and discontinuities of this love, the work establishes a common framework by which to appreciate these major philosophers and their work. This book analyzes philosophical love in the very works and arguments of the philosophers, in their search and clarification of what to them stands for wisdom. Philosophical love is analyzed insofar as this love produces results, insofar as this love tries to come to terms with its proper goal.

∽

First, this book analyzes some of the major philosophers insofar as their texts manifest their philosophical love, as well as the transformation of this love at the hands of these historical figures. Secondly, as a natural outgrowth of the analysis of philosophical love among the various philosophers, the book seeks to identify the vital source(s) of philosophy in the human being, the root(s) of philosophical love in human existence. The various thinkers included in this book were selected because each of them provides an illuminating perspective on the significance of philosophical love, while together they support a balanced discussion of the topic. Their selection is meant to inform the reader's own understanding and appreciation of philosophical love as a vital, and therefore personal, human drive. The varied, developed expressions of this love among the major thinkers help us orient our own philosophical interests and see the significance of philosophy in human life.

This book does not pretend to provide a treatment of all the different forms of philosophical desire, or an exhaustive textual and historical analysis of the periods and thinkers included here. It draws conclusions about ancient, medieval, and modern philosophical desire based only on some of the outstanding representatives of these periods. Several major philosophers and schools of philosophy are not included. What this book does provide is a sufficient spectrum of philosophies to begin to approach the question of philosophical desire in context and with some depth. For, above all, the goal of this book is to provide a distinctive approach to philosophy—not one to replace all other approaches, but one that can enrich our study of philosophers as well as our understanding of ourselves as students of philosophy. This approach focuses and reflects on the vital sources of philosophical endeavor, specifically the desires that ground philosophical activity.[2] Naturally, considering the limited material developed in this study, this work and its approach can only be a beginning, an introduction. At the same time, this contribution does advance to the discussion of the fundamental issues, and therefore can carry the reader well along the path of exploring these questions.

In focusing on the fundamental origins of philosophy and philosophies, and in developing these origins as principles that generate philosophical outlooks, this work also explains the basic ideas and positions of the philosophers included. Accordingly, this book can serve as an introduction to Western philosophy. However, through its own approach, this book also has something to offer to the student or scholar who is already familiar with these major thinkers.[3]

One more thing should be mentioned briefly at this point. As shall be seen, some versions of philosophical love are broader and more comprehensive, while others are more specialized or particularized. Not surprisingly, considering the above-mentioned specialization proper to modern times, the ancient and medieval versions of love of wisdom are broader than the modern expressions of philosophical love, in the following sense. Ancient and medieval thinkers understood and developed love of wisdom as a comprehensive desire engaging both the character and the intellect. On the other hand, modern philosophers tend to base their pursuits on more fragmented or particularized drives of the human self. Even though there is great variety among ancient and medieval thinkers, as well as among

2. This approach is already found in Flores, "The Roots of Love of Wisdom," 623–40.

3. For these reasons, this book is different from other studies on the origins and nature of philosophy, such as Hadot's *Philosophy as a Way of Life* and Pieper's *Leisure, the Basis of Culture*. Hadot focuses mainly on the behavior and actual practices of philosophers, while Pieper concentrates on leisure and its dimensions.

modern ones, this basic distinction is now mentioned in order to highlight the fundamental issue at stake in the investigation that follows.

Is philosophy fundamentally a comprehensive desire rooted in the essential core of the human being, a desire that therefore seeks the general fulfillment of this core? If so, what is this core, and how does philosophy try to fulfill it? Or, is philosophy a specialized activity rooted in some particular human desire (which may even vary according to the philosopher), in a desire disengaged from other, fundamentally human exigencies and dimensions? If so, how does this particular desire justify and satisfy itself through the philosophy it produces? Perhaps the alternatives suggested by these questions are options for us to choose, options with crucial implications.

As shall be shown, philosophers provide different answers to these questions, through their own aspirations and accomplishments, even if they may not formulate these questions explicitly or on these terms. Moreover, they can help us arrive at our own answers. The answers to these questions have implications about the significance of philosophical activity in human life, and about the type of fulfillment that this activity can provide to human beings. Accordingly, this exploration of human desire should enhance our understanding of philosophy and of ourselves, and make us better prepared to orient our own drives and aspirations.

However, the concrete assessment of these various philosophical alternatives and their significance can take place only through direct engagement with the philosophers themselves, to whom we now turn.

Chapter 1

Ancient Greek Love of Wisdom

As students of philosophy know, the word *philosophy* means literally love of wisdom. *Philosophia*, the Greek word for philosophy, is composed of two notions, namely, *philia*, which means love, and *sophia*, which means wisdom. This literal meaning also indicates its original and deeper meaning. Philosophy, as it comes to life in ancient Greece, meant the pursuit of wisdom, the human activity engaged in seeking wisdom. At first, philosophy was not a set of doctrines, or a profession, or an academic subject, or even wisdom as such. According to the original lovers of wisdom, philosophy never can be identical to wisdom, because wisdom is primarily knowledge of divine, eternal things. Mortals, by definition, cannot fully assimilate divine things, since these things transcend them.[1] They can only work towards an ever more adequate understanding of the divine and eternal. This conviction is shared by many ancient philosophers, including Socrates (469–399 BC), his student Plato (ca. 429–347 BC), and Plato's student Aristotle (384–322 BC). Among the thinkers who lived before Socrates (the so-called Presocratics), Pythagoras of Samos (ca. 570–494 BC) is reputedly the first to call himself a philosopher, rather than a sage or wise man (*sophos*).

These Greek philosophers, as lovers of wisdom, distinguish themselves from the Greek sophists, who see themselves as already wise. The term *sophist* includes etymologically only the notion of wisdom (*sophia*)

---

1. See, for example, Plato, *Phaedo* 66e; Aristotle, *Metaphysics* 1.2.982b28–983 a11; Aristotle, *Nicomachean Ethics* 10.7.1177b26–35.

1

and lacks the notion of love (*philia*) included in the term *philosopher*. According to the sophist, human beings can be possessors of wisdom. For Protagoras (ca. 490–420 BC), the paradigm of Greek sophists, wisdom can be the property of human beings because, as he puts it, man is the measure of all things.[2] This means, for Protagoras, that truth is equivalent to appearance, and so every human being is able to judge accurately what appears to him or her. In this sense, every individual is as wise as another. Protagoras' concept of wisdom is different from the philosophical concept of wisdom. For Protagoras, wisdom is a wholly human affair, without reference to the divine.

However, there is a sense in which a human being can be wiser than another, according to Protagoras. Since truth is appearance, wisdom in the strict sense is the control of appearances, especially through rhetoric and argument, in order to make one's own judgment or "wisdom" prevail. The ultimate goal of wisdom is, therefore, success in practical affairs. These ancient Greek sophists were professional teachers who traveled from town to town, teaching young men their way to achieve worldly success, and charging good money for it. This understanding of wisdom as the art of manipulation earns the term *sophistry* its negative connotations in later history,[3] even if the reality indicated by the term still thrives, often with a great deal of prestige.

On the other hand, the philosophers, such as Socrates, Plato, and Aristotle, do not value wisdom only in practical or utilitarian terms, and they certainly do not conceive of the practical benefits of wisdom in Protagoras' terms. Rather, to the philosophers, wisdom is fundamentally desirable for its own sake, even if wisdom entails practical benefits. To them, seeking wisdom is the highest expression of human freedom. Of all the human activities, the pursuit of wisdom is the best precisely because it is the freest. At the same time, wisdom is the highest form of knowledge because it is the freest form of knowledge.[4]

Human beings think and use knowledge in all areas of life—in speaking, tilling the soil, riding horses, building ships, etc. Certainly, some

2. Curd, *Presocratics Reader*, 98. Like virtually all Presocratics, Protagoras' positions are known through the writings of other authors. The following rendition of Protagoras relies primarily on Plato's *Theaetetus* 152a–c; 166a–168c.

3. Plato's definition of the sophist, at the very end of his *Sophist* (268d), already captures succinctly some of the disreputable qualities associated with the term.

4. The clearest expression of this is perhaps that of Aristotle in *Metaphysics* 1.2.982a30–b3; b17–27. See also Plato, *Theaetetus* 172d–176a.

human beings think better than others, know more than others, and use knowledge better than others, but all human beings engage in thinking and knowing, capacities that characterize the mind and define human life. However, in most activities, thinking and knowing serve some ulterior purpose, such as growing food, providing shelter, or obtaining some pleasure. In these activities, thinking and knowing are subservient to something else, such as the various needs of the body; the human mind is not strictly free, since it is employed as a means to some ulterior end.

On the other hand, the freedom of the mind or soul would have to consist in the pursuit of its proper end, an end that it seeks and values for its own sake. For the original lovers of wisdom, the proper goal and fulfillment of the mind must correspond to its essence—an entity that thinks, questions, and investigates. Hence, the proper goal of the mind (and of human nature, if indeed the mind is the commanding and defining aspect of human life) consists in the acquisition of free rather than servile knowledge. And only in pursuing knowledge for its own sake is the mind freely pursuing its proper end, dictating its own course of action, and seeking its own kind of satisfaction. Naturally, this interest in knowledge as such becomes a search for the greatest and best form of knowledge, for knowledge of the most important things. This knowledge is wisdom, and philosophy is the dedication to wisdom.

Philosophy, therefore, originates in freedom. This is possible when human beings possess the leisure, as well as the requisite dispositions, habits, and education, to engage in the free pursuit of knowledge. Human beings who must toil simply to procure the necessities of life have no time for philosophy. Human beings dedicated to the pursuit of wealth and power have no time for philosophy, and probably no interest in it. Human beings who constantly seek the gratification of their appetites or passions have no capacity for philosophy. Human beings with little intellectual talent or deficient educations will not be well equipped for the pursuit of wisdom. Finally, human beings who engage in the study of philosophical ideas for purposes other than wisdom itself are not true philosophers. In short, engaging in philosophy genuinely is very difficult.

Moreover, the possession of these prerequisites is not sufficient for the pursuit of wisdom. In addition to them, the essential component must be present—a powerful love of wisdom. What is the source and nature of this love? To answer this question specifically, we must look at how this love manifests itself in different philosophers. However, one common factor associated with the origin of love of wisdom, according to the Greek philosophers, is wonder. Philosophy, they say, begins in wonder.[5] The experience of wonder provides a pure motivation for knowledge, since wonder seeks fulfillment in knowledge as such. However, as we shall see throughout this book, the concrete expression of love of wisdom entails various dimensions, and this expression varies among philosophers.

∾

The ancient Greek philosophers recognized that philosophy is the most fulfilling and freest of all human activities. To them, philosophy is the activity through which the highest human faculty works freely towards its own fulfillment. Philosophy, as the freest pursuit, is also the least necessary, but it is the noblest, since it the highest calling of the highest faculty. For this reason, philosophy is the highest form of desire or love, which seeks the highest form of human fulfillment.

Philosophy, in this ancient Greek sense, is difficult not only because freedom is difficult to obtain; the vast majority of human beings are occupied by so many necessities and (nonphilosophical) desires. Philosophy is intrinsically difficult because seeking knowledge for its own sake is also seeking the highest form of knowledge, which is knowledge of the ultimate truths. As the ancient Greek philosophers quickly recognized, human beings are not the highest beings in the universe. To them, wisdom concerns itself primarily with divine, eternal things, which transcend humanity. The ultimate reason, therefore, why human beings cannot possess wisdom fully has to do with the very place of human beings in the universe. Mortals, as such, are incapable of assimilating fully what exceeds them. At the same time, to these Greek thinkers, approaching the divine is the greatest human calling and fulfillment.

Socrates, Plato, and Aristotle share, in general outline, this view of the nature and goal of philosophy. They understand themselves, in being lovers of wisdom, as answering to the highest human calling. In addition, they understand their calling and activity as genuine freedom. The three would say that philosophy begins in wonder. Finally, the three understand wisdom in reference to the divine. However, even though the drive that fuels their activity springs from the same general source—from the soul's desire to fulfill its highest calling—they interpret and develop this source in different ways. Their different loves for wisdom give us three fertile and

---

5. Plato, *Theaetetus* 155d; Aristotle, *Metaphysics* 1.2.982b11–22.

4

influential ways to develop the philosophical drive that springs from the core of the human being.

Developing this topic requires more than analyzing how terms such as *love, wisdom, philosophy,* and *love of wisdom* appear in texts. For the present motivation is not the question of a nominal definition. Philosophy or love of wisdom, as understood by Socrates, Plato, and Aristotle, is the highest human calling. Their respective loves for wisdom reveal their interpretation and development of this calling, and their views regarding its ultimate purpose. This requires a look at some of their fundamental principles.

I.1
SOCRATES AND THE DESIRE FOR SELF-KNOWLEDGE

Socrates is famous for saying that he knows nothing, that his reputation for wisdom stems from his awareness of his own ignorance, unlike most people, who think they know what they really do not know. Against this background, it is rather surprising that in Plato's *Symposium* Socrates boldly claims that the one thing he does know is love.[6] Socrates' knowledge of love, specifically love of wisdom, is mentioned in other Platonic texts as well. A couple of questions impose themselves. Why is love the one thing Socrates, that paradigm of the philosopher, claims to know? What is the nature of Socrates' love of wisdom?

As students of Greek philosophy know, distinguishing Socrates' philosophy from Plato's is not simple, since Plato wrote most of the documents we possess regarding Socrates, and Socrates appears in the vast majority of Plato's dialogues. At the same time, scholars generally agree in calling a group of Plato's dialogues "Socratic dialogues" since they are closest to the original Socrates. Moreover, among these Socratic dialogues, Plato's *Apology* is probably the most accurate portrayal of the historical Socrates.[7] Accordingly, Socrates' description of his philosophical activity in the *Apology* will be our chief indication of his love of wisdom.

In the *Apology*, Socrates presents his defense to the Athenian assembly against the charges that eventually lead to his condemnation and death. Even though in the *Apology* Socrates is being indicted for specific charges, namely, for corrupting the Athenian youth as well as for impiety (not believing in the traditional gods), Socrates provides a broader defense. Socrates'

6. Plato, *Symposium* 177e.

7. See the introduction to the *Apology* by Grube, in Plato, *Five Dialogues*, 21.

defense is twofold, since (as he claims) his accusers are twofold, namely, his early accusers and his recent accusers (those who bring him to trial in the *Apology*, a group headed by Meletus). By damaging his reputation in Athens, his early accusers, according to Socrates, provided background and strength to his recent accusers, since many Athenians (including many in the assembly) now share an old and ingrained bias against Socrates. These early accusers complained that Socrates does wrong in "studying things in the sky and below the earth," that "he makes the worse into the stronger argument, and he teaches these same things to others."[8]

In his defense, Socrates maintains that his primary interest has been virtue,[9] not things in the sky and below the earth—not the investigation and teaching of theological and cosmological matters. He also distinguishes himself from the sophists, who more legitimately could be accused of making the worse into the stronger argument. Although like the sophists Socrates is an expert arguer, he uses arguments for a different end—to make others aware of their own ignorance, a necessary step towards the virtuous life. For the consciousness of ignorance and the experience of wonder and perplexity prompt us to improve our minds and seek wisdom. Socrates is further distinguished from the sophists in that he does not charge a fee to those who listen to him and converse with him. He is poor after all. Moreover, Socrates claims that he does not teach, strictly speaking, since he is himself ignorant. Since he does not teach in the sense of imposing doctrines, he is not guilty of corrupting the young, and even less of disseminating impious theological and cosmological views.

Socrates also tells us about the origins of the philosophical activity that made him famous in history as well as unpopular in Athens. Interestingly, these origins indicate that Socrates was genuinely religious, in his own way.[10] Socrates' friend Chaerephon once asked the oracle at Delphi, shrine of Apollo, if there was a man wiser than Socrates. The god's oracle, delivered through his priestess, the Pythia, said that no one was wiser than Socrates.[11] Baffled by this answer, since Socrates did not think he was wise

---

8. *Apology* 19c.

9. In *Phaedo* 96a–e, Socrates mentions that as a young man he was interested in natural philosophy.

10. About his calling and mission as a philosopher, Socrates reportedly said, "To do this has, as I say, been enjoined upon me by the god, by means of oracles and dreams, and in every other way that a divine manifestation has ever ordered a man to do anything" (*Apology* 33c).

11. *Apology* 21a.

and at the same time he could not believe that the god was lying, Socrates proceeded to investigate the meaning of the god's response. His investigation became the examination, through dialogue, of those with a reputation for wisdom in Athens, namely, the politicians, the poets, and the craftsmen. Socrates wanted to see for himself if no one in Athens was wiser than he.

Concerning the politicians, Socrates discovered that they could not give a satisfactory account of what they claimed to know, presumably basic principles of government and legislation, such as the nature of justice and virtue, even though they thought that they possessed knowledge of these things. Concerning the poets, although they could produce inspirational works, they too (often to their own surprise) could not give an adequate account of basic themes in their works, such as wisdom, piety, and courage. Unlike the politicians and the poets, the craftsmen did possess know-how in their respective crafts and could give an account of why a craft proceeds through certain steps and not others in order to produce the desired result. However, Socrates noticed a severe deficiency in the craftsmen: their specific expertise led them to assume they were already wise without qualification. Hence, they neglected cultivating the most worthy expertise, which is not excellence as a carpenter or shipbuilder but rather excellence as a human being. Generally, Socrates' interlocutors confused success with wisdom; satisfied with their success and good reputation, they assumed they were wise when they were not.[12] Many (if not most) of Socrates' interlocutors resented rather than appreciated that their ignorance was revealed.

I.1a
Socrates' Program

Socrates' investigation into the meaning of the oracle translated into a philosophical program, to be carried out through dialogue (there are no writings left by Socrates) with his fellow Athenian citizens. After his investigation, what does Socrates conclude? What the god meant, in saying Socrates was wisest, is that human wisdom as such is weak and that, therefore, the wisest human being is the one who, like Socrates, is aware of his fundamental ignorance. Moreover, the god intends Socrates to perform a fundamental political function in Athens[13]—to examine himself and others about the

---

12. Ibid., 22d–e.
13. Ibid., 23b.

most important questions, namely, those concerning human virtue, the best state of the human soul and the best way of life for a human being.

These are the most important questions for a human being for two reasons. First, these questions address the real human self, the thinking self or soul, which includes the moral character, since the soul not only forms opinions but also intends and acts. The question of what makes a good or a bad person, simply speaking, is far more important than the question of what makes a person good or bad in a certain respect, such as what makes a good or a bad lyre player. Even though many persons place great emphasis on the acquisition of wealth, prestige, and power, these interests have little to do with that which is properly human, namely, the soul, and even distract the soul from cultivating itself. What good is it to have opportunities if one lacks the physical health by which to take advantage of them? Even more to the point, what good is it to have external goods if one's very soul, that by which one lives, is ruined with ignorance and vice? Socratic self-examination cultivates the true self, and so essentially aims at true excellence and true happiness. Ironically, this path towards true fulfillment makes many resentful and angry. That is why, in the *Apology*, which records how he is condemned and put to death by the majority, Socrates can still say to the Athenian people, "I make you be happy."[14]

Secondly, these questions are most important since they are decisive for human life. Since they concern the true self, they concern what is under our control. We have little ability to control "things in the sky and below the earth." Ultimately, we are not able to control our fortunes, or how others will perceive and treat us. However, we can learn to control what pertains to our true self, namely, our reason and character. We can decide to act well or badly and to follow a good or a bad life. For Socrates, the soul as such cannot be harmed except by the soul itself.[15] Many things can affect our bodies and possessions. However, unless the soul itself permits it, nothing can affect the soul's own virtue, its own values and convictions, as well as its power to take its own stance in the face of fortune and circumstance. The more virtuous a soul is, the freer it is, since virtue is the soul's self-rule, its ability to obey its own reason, rather than mere opinions, feelings, or appetites.

Moreover, as far as death is concerned, human beings posses no evidence to judge it as a good or bad thing. However, human beings do have

14. Ibid., 36e.

15. See ibid., 30d, where this is implied.

access to themselves, and they can learn to recognize their own strengths and deficiencies, and whether one course of action is more virtuous than another. This is the basis of two of Socrates' famous sayings: that it is better to suffer than to do injustice,[16] and that virtuous living is more important than living per se (sometimes choosing virtue comes at the expense of death).[17]

As to the first saying, to suffer injustice is to suffer external damage (damage to what belongs to us, such as our bodies or possessions), not damage to one's very self. On the other hand, the soul does become worse by doing injustice, by living and acting badly, since through these things the soul becomes less able to rule itself, to obey reason rather than lower impulses. Hence, the guide to human life and action must be the knowledge of virtue and vice, of good and bad, rather than considerations of life and death. The soul should base itself on what is proper to it, namely, knowledge, rather than on matters concerning which the soul has no knowledge, such as whether death is a good or a bad thing. Who knows conclusively what happens after death? However, to some extent, the soul has the ability to distinguish between good and bad, between virtue and vice. It may seem strange to some, but the safer route, according to Socrates, is to follow virtue even if it means dying, since following virtue is always beneficial to the soul. This is the basis of his second saying.

To Socrates, those who want to harm him by unjustly condemning him are harming themselves more than they are harming him. For the same reason, if the assembly would offer to pardon Socrates' life on the condition that he would stop practicing philosophy, Socrates would refuse. For philosophy is the pursuit of virtue and wisdom.[18] Socrates even tells those who resent him and want to kill him that he would be satisfied if they would take "revenge" upon him by subjecting his own children to the same examination he practiced.[19] Socrates is consistent; he does what he prescribes.

Moreover, even though human wisdom is weak, we can learn to know ourselves and become aware of our ignorance, our vices and, consequently, what we need to work towards. We can learn to become lovers of wisdom.

16. Ibid.

17. *Crito* 48b.

18. Concerning conduct, Socrates is very influential in Hellenistic philosophy, especially Stoicism.

19. *Apology* 41e–42a.

In order to become masters of ourselves and lovers of wisdom, the soul first needs to be made mindful of its own condition and relative worth. Moreover, living virtuously is always a work in progress; the soul needs constant practice. Just as physical health depends on a regular regimen of diet and exercise, achieving and preserving the virtue of the soul depends on the proper moral and intellectual regimen. That is why, in the *Apology*, Socrates claims that the greatest good for a human being is to discuss virtue every day.[20]

Socrates' examination targets the true self, namely, the soul—the principle that thinks, decides, and rules the body. Accordingly, this examination improves human beings in the highest sense. How does it improve them? First, this examination lays the soul bare. The examination aims to bring to light and show to the interlocutors (and to any witnesses) the adequacy of the soul in question. In examining whether the opinions held by the soul are true or false, Socrates also examines whether this soul's view of itself as possessor of wisdom is true or false. The very worth of the soul is under question. (This could be enough, it would seem, for some to want to be rid of him.) For virtue depends on self-knowledge, on the awareness of one's deficiencies and, concomitantly, on one's genuine love of wisdom. Socrates' philosophical activity aims at uncovering the true self so that this self can behold its own condition and desire improvement.[21]

Socrates, the wisest man in Athens due to his understanding of his ignorance, the consummate lover of wisdom, devotes his life to the dissemination, not of wisdom or knowledge, but of love. Socrates' goal is to make others into lovers like him. His love of wisdom contains a fundamental civic spirit. In being a lover of wisdom, Socrates is also a lover of his city and of humanity. In Plato's *Crito*, his friend Crito urges him to escape from prison, where he is waiting for execution after his trial. However, Socrates argues that reason dictates that he must obey his sentence. For it is never right to commit wrong. To escape, after agreeing to live his whole life as a citizen of Athens, and after presenting his defense on his own terms to the assembly, would be to commit wrong by violating the city's laws, which deserve more reverence than one's parents and family, since they are the

---

20. Ibid., 38a.

21. This helps explain Socrates' profound impact on his contemporaries. Part of this impact, however, was the resentment some felt towards Socrates for being "uncovered" by him. Socrates claims that the reason why many want to kill him is that they want to avoid giving an account of their lives. See ibid., 39c.

very principle of organized life.[22] Moreover, to escape just to save his own life would undermine Socrates' own principles, such as his commitment to the good life (the philosophical life) rather than to life simply, which to Socrates is inseparable from his role as a citizen.

Socrates even claims (as mentioned) that his philosophical occupation is an act of obedience to the god: the god wants him to perform that social function in Athens, the function of promoting human excellence. Socrates is meant to wake up Athens, like a gadfly that stirs up a powerful but sluggish horse, by prompting the citizens to examine themselves, even if they get annoyed at him and want to be rid of him, like the horse swatting at the pesky gadfly with its tail.[23] For Socrates, philosophy is an interpersonal project. For the soul comes to know itself through dialogue. That is why Socrates questions his fellow citizens individually and refuses to give speeches to the crowd. Each soul has its own strengths and weaknesses, its own background and way of thinking. To lay the soul bare, to see its condition clearly, each soul must be examined on its own terms.

I.1b
Ignorance and Love

Socrates is famous for claiming that his wisdom consists in knowing that he does not know. This also means that his wisdom consists in the knowledge, not of wisdom, but of the love of wisdom, since his ignorance grounds his lifelong pursuit of virtue and wisdom. Even though Socrates is not wise in the strict sense, he is cultivated to the point that he possesses a good idea of the requirements for knowledge, as well as exceptional argumentative skill. He is an expert at examining his interlocutors and bringing them further along the path towards knowledge by helping them question, refine, or develop their own claims.[24] Usually, this includes the experience of doubting that which was at first taken for granted—the experience of perplexity and wonder, which is the beginning of love of wisdom. However, only very few of his interlocutors become lovers of wisdom, people who make the pursuit of the most important questions their primary activity and concern.

22. *Crito* 50b–54d.

23. *Apology* 30e–31b.

24. Plato likens Socrates to a midwife, since Socrates helps his interlocutors deliver the offspring of their souls, namely, their opinions. See *Theaetetus* 149a–151d.

Socrates' wisdom also consists in knowing that human wisdom as such is quite weak. Wisdom, strictly speaking, belongs to the gods. At the same time, while reading his interventions in Plato's relevant texts, it is difficult sometimes to take seriously his claim that he knows nothing or very little, and that human wisdom consists in knowing this (as the oracle seems to claim in saying Socrates is wisest). In what sense are human beings fundamentally ignorant? Indeed, even though human beings have access to myths and stories, human beings through reason alone cannot establish infallible conclusions regarding the gods and the significance of death. On the other hand, human beings are not ignorant in an absolute sense. After all, the craftsmen know many useful things, as Socrates recognizes, and the politicians and the poets know how to achieve many things.

Socrates' claim that he is ignorant should be understood in the context of his philosophical program: Socrates is ignorant about the most important human questions, namely, wisdom and virtue. The following qualification is also necessary: Socrates knows love. He is in love with wisdom and can make others fall in love with wisdom, or at least catch a glimpse of the initial spark of this love, through the experience of wonder. Moreover, Socrates *knows how* to pursue wisdom in himself and others, which includes a special and powerful rational skill.

However, even with these qualifications, it is difficult to believe at face value Socrates' ignorance of wisdom and virtue, as one sees him expertly guiding his interlocutors through a maze of complexities, illuminating their deficiencies and encouraging new and more vigorous attempts (which, even if unsuccessful, at least strengthen the soul). Sometimes, he seems like an expert craftsman who refuses to reveal answers to his apprentice but nevertheless guides him through questions. Nevertheless, one must recognize that Socrates is ultimately ignorant. For, absolutely speaking, he does not possess wisdom or virtue, even though he is an expert seeker or lover of wisdom and virtue. In the latter sense, he is like an expert craftsman, since he knows how to pursue wisdom. Unlike an expert craftsman who can know the form and function of his works, however, Socrates does not possess fully wisdom itself and virtue itself, for the following reason.

Socrates is wise only insofar as he is a lover of wisdom, and not wise absolutely speaking, since human excellence (like bodily health) requires constant cultivation, lifelong practice. Human wisdom, therefore, is equivalent to the commitment to pursue wisdom throughout life. This active pursuit naturally improves the soul, and so the soul becomes wise in the sense that it becomes *wiser*, but not wise in an absolute sense. After all, living is an active process that demands interaction, adaptation, and exertion and that always permits improvement. Even the things we come to understand need to be rethought and reformulated (and often revised) every time we try to clarify or explain them. Human virtue and wisdom exist insofar as human beings pursue and cultivate them; they cannot exist for human beings as fixed, immutable states. Eternal and perfect wisdom would be divine, not human. Accordingly, the goal of Socrates' philosophy is not theoretical knowledge without moral or practical knowledge. The pursuit of wisdom is a way of life that must cultivate understanding as well as conduct. Socrates is famous, and often misunderstood, for his reputed claim that virtue is equivalent to knowledge.[25] However, his point is not that the theoretical understanding of the definition of virtue, however difficult this goal might be, is sufficient for the virtuous life. Rather, his point is that only the knowledge of virtue that can give an account of itself, *and* influence one's conduct, is genuine. After all, Socrates' primary theoretical activity, namely discussion, was also a social activity, and as such it had a practical dimension. This is not to say that Socrates confuses thinking and action; discussing the nature of courage is one thing, acting courageously in battle another (even if discussing the nature of courage is in some sense courageous, and acting courageously requires some understanding of courage).

I.1c
The Socratic Question

An important aspect of Socrates' love of wisdom, probably the one for which he is most famous, since it becomes central in Plato, has to do with the type of questions he asks. Socrates asks such questions as, what is piety? What is courage? What is justice? In focusing on *what* a given thing is, he is searching for an account of the form, the essence or nature: the one principle through which the many instances are included within a class. In the case of piety (the topic of Plato's *Euthyphro*), he is searching for an account of piety itself—that which all pious things share insofar as they are pious, and makes all of them pious. In searching for the form, he is also searching for an account of the one and true standard by which human

---

25. This claim is suggested in Plato, *Protagoras* 357c–360e. Aristotle comments on this claim in *Nicomachean Ethics* 6.13.1144b26–29.

beings can judge correctly a given thing as pious.[26] Human beings do call certain actions pious and other actions impious. They may even compare different pious actions with each other and decide that some of them are more pious than others. This is true not only in regard to piety but also in regard to virtue and vice in general (as well as other things, such as beauty); human beings call some things right and others wrong, some better and others worse. If human beings pass judgment regarding virtue and vice, the question presents itself: What is the basis of their judgment? Is there a fundamentally correct basis for passing such a judgment? According to Socrates, human beings should try to base their judgments and decisions regarding virtue (and vice) on the knowledge of virtue itself, rather than on the mere appearance of virtue (and certainly not on mere emotion or appetite).

The form is not only the principle through which instances are included in a class. The form is also the principle by which we know these instances as instances of the form. For example, when we judge that an action is courageous (or when we compare different actions on the basis of courage), we are also assuming that we recognize the principle by which the given action is courageous. For to call the action courageous is also to include it within the class of courageous things, and including it within this class presupposes the use of some principle by which to include it. Moreover, this use is based on our assumption that we possess some knowledge of the principle. In brief, in judging that a particular action is courageous, we are also claiming implicitly that we possess some understanding of courage itself, some understanding of the principle—the form—by which all courageous things are courageous, some understanding of that which all courageous things share insofar as they are courageous.

The question now is whether the assumption on which our judgment is based, namely, that we know this principle, is legitimate. The question is whether we really know courage itself. After all, it could be that our judgment is based merely on some prejudice or on some faulty notion. How can we know if our appeal to knowledge is solid? We can try to give a consistent account of courage itself. In other words, we can engage in a Socratic discussion. The result of these discussions is, more often than not, that we have to refine, revise, or rethink what we thought we knew, that what we thought we knew does not exactly correspond to what we actually do know.

---

26. *Euthyphro* 6e.

Since everybody passes judgment regarding right and wrong, good and bad, etc., everybody may be engaged in a Socratic discussion. Even a child who accuses another of not playing fairly may be asked legitimately, what is fairness? After all, in accusing another of not exhibiting this trait, the child is also implicitly claiming that he knows this trait, at least to the extent that he can recognize it. In this case, the accusation could be legitimate, if it is based on some understanding that playing fairly means that the same rules apply to both children, and the other child disregarded the rules. However, it could be that the accusation is illegitimate, if it is based, for example, on the caprice that loosing in a game means that the other child must be playing unfairly, and on this occasion the other child won. Only some conversation can reveal whether the child is basing his judgment on some legitimate recognition of what is fair, or on some caprice, emotion, or appearance. Moreover, this type of conversation is beneficial, since it makes the child better able to use his reason as the ruling principle of his judgments and actions.

The form itself that is searched in these Socratic discussions is unique. For example, there cannot be two or more forms of piety since piety is that which all pious things have in common. Two or more types or "forms" of piety would still share piety; hence, the piety that they share would be the one and true form of piety. Since the form is one and not many, it is also changeless. If the form would cease to be, all the instances of the form would also have to cease to be, since the form is the principle through which the instances belong to the given class. If the form would vary, the instances also would have to vary; they would not manifest any consistent common features, and there would be no basis for knowledge at all.[27]

Socrates' emphasis on forms, like the rest of his activity, seems to center on virtue and the love of wisdom. Discussing these forms benefits the soul, since the soul's excellence depends on the cultivation of reason and knowledge, on the pursuit of truth for its own sake. Ideally, the soul should be able to ground its judgments and actions on some understanding of the principles of knowledge, the forms, even if this understanding always can be improved. For only by guiding our lives through rational examination are we living freely, living the life that is proper to us, namely, the good life.

However, we cannot be sure about the extent to which Socrates himself engaged in questions concerning the being of the forms, the function

27. Perhaps some questions or problems cannot be resolved because there is no form to be found, but this would still require thorough examination.

of the forms in human knowledge, and the relation between the forms and the instances of the forms. Nor can we be completely sure about doctrines he may have held concerning these questions. Plato expresses, through the character of Socrates, definite positions on the forms, but these positions are associated with Plato himself rather than with the historical Socrates. It is in the context of these positions that we discover Plato's own approach to love of wisdom. Plato's love of wisdom emphasizes many aspects of the philosophy of Socrates (which survives mainly because of Plato), notably wonder, learned ignorance, virtue, and discussion on forms (after all, Plato wrote dialogues). Like Socrates, Plato emphasizes that love of wisdom is the highest and freest desire of the soul and that, therefore, the pursuit of virtue and wisdom is the best form of human fulfillment. Plato, like Socrates, recognizes that love of wisdom is grounded in the core of the self and aims at the fulfillment of this core. Moreover, he recognizes that this core includes both reason and character, thinking and conduct. Hence, love of wisdom, in Socrates as well as in Plato, is genuinely a complete love, a love stemming from the human essence as a whole, which therefore aims at complete fulfillment.

However, Plato also develops love of wisdom in an original way. Platonic love of wisdom interprets and grounds itself on new principles, giving a whole new meaning to this core human drive. It is to Plato's own love of wisdom that we now turn.

I.2
PLATO'S LOVE OF WISDOM: DESIRE FOR LIBERATION THAT REACHES THE DIVINE

Love of wisdom in Plato is, ultimately, the drive of the soul to reach its own proper destination. This destination, which is divine, is the soul's source as well as its sustaining principle. Love of wisdom is a drive for freedom, in two related senses. The soul seeks to rule itself. The soul also seeks liberation from the dimensions that obscure its path towards its proper destination.

I.2a
The Forms and the Soul

Plato's analysis of forms leads to his position that forms are transcendent principles both of the soul and of the world we experience. Plato analyzes not only forms pertaining to virtues specifically but also forms that pertain to the order, beauty, and intelligibility of the world, such as equality, beauty, and the good (the highest form).[28] In brief, the forms in Plato are metaphysical principles, as well as principles of knowledge.

In the *Phaedo*, Plato's version of Socrates' last conversation and death, Plato provides a developed treatment of the forms and the soul's immortality.[29] The first and crucial step in this dialogue is the recognition that the mind, in its judgment of sensible things, appeals to transcendent principles, to principles that are neither available in the world of the senses nor reducible to this world.

Plato makes this point while analyzing the form of equality.[30] We recognize that some things are equal in certain respects. For example, two sticks are equal insofar as they are sticks, and other things are equal in other respects. We can also recognize, for example, that two brown sticks are equal in more respects than two sticks of different colors, since the two brown sticks are equal insofar as they are sticks and insofar as they are brown, while the sticks of different colors are equal only insofar as they are sticks. In other words, the mind recognizes greater equality among some things than among other things. At the same time, the mind recognizes that any type of equality exhibited by sensible things is always limited equality. No two sensible things are equal absolutely, since there is always some difference that distinguishes the one thing from the other thing. However, some set of things displays equality in more respects, more completely, than another set of things. We may say that some set of things is closer to absolute equality than another set of things, even if the notion of absolute equality is not completely clear to us. However, in order to recognize this fact, the mind must have at least some connection with absolute equality.

The mind judges sensible equality in reference to absolute equality (otherwise it would never recognize deficiencies in terms of equality), which does not and cannot appear in the world of the senses. For every sensible thing is distinct; an equal sensible thing is also, by definition, unequal in some respect. Nothing sensible, therefore, can be the Equal itself,

28. Plato had many interests, including things "in the sky and below the earth," as we can see from his scientific and cosmological treatments. However, the soul is central in his philosophy.

29. The influence of Pythagoras—who emphasized mathematical principles of reality, the immortality of the soul and its need for purification in this life—is evident in this dialogue. See the introduction to *Phaedo* by Cooper, in Plato, *Five Dialogues*, 93–94.

30. *Phaedo* 74a–76e.

the form of equality. On the other hand, equality (and the other forms) cannot be sensible, by their very nature. The mind recognizes sensible equality in the light of absolute equality, which is one and unchanging (unlike the variety of equal, sensible things that change). Absolute equality must be one since it is the ultimate principle of all equality, the ultimate unity of equality to which all the variety of equal things is traced back. This principle must be also unchanging, since it is an absolute unity of equality, the very identity of equality, which remains always itself. Accordingly, equality itself is not only the principle of the knowledge of equality but also the principle of equal sensible things. The same thing may be said about beauty itself and beautiful things, goodness itself and good things, etc.

Accordingly, only the forms are true being and, therefore, only knowledge of the forms is genuine knowledge. Sensible things, which are many and changing, can be known only to the extent to which they are influenced by the unchanging forms, to the extent to which they exhibit the unity and identity of their principles. Sensible things belong, properly speaking, to the realm of becoming, not to the realm of being. In terms of cognition, therefore, we can have opinions regarding sensible things, but not knowledge in the strict sense of the word. The sensible world is intelligible and ordered ultimately because it depends on purely intelligible principles, the forms. Moreover, the interpretation of the sensible world is adequate to the extent that it is in reference to these intelligible principles. For sensible things are, ultimately, copies of the forms. The sensible world owes its being to the forms, and the forms give being to the sensible world.

The Good is Plato's first principle of being and knowledge.[31] The different forms, such as equality and justice, presuppose one principle, a form of forms. For even though each form is unique, each form still shares something with other forms, namely, formal being. Equality and justice are each purely one and unchanging. But they share the very fact that they are forms; they share their formal being. Accordingly, just as the variety of equal things is traced back to Equality itself, the various forms are themselves traced back to the One principle that gives them their formal being. This principle is the Good, the principle that gives being to intelligible and, thereby, to sensible reality. It is properly called the Good, since it gives of itself. The Good is a creative principle, and the sensible world, according to Plato, owes its being ultimately to this creator.[32] The Good is to the

---

31. *Republic* 507a–511e.

32. See also *Timaeus* 29e–30a. However, Plato's account of the nature of creation is a separate study.

intelligible realm what the sun is to the visible realm. Sight can see what is actually visible, visible colors, only when light is present. Similarly, the soul can understand what is actually intelligible, the forms, only because these forms possess true being given to them by the Good. Accordingly, the Good is the first principle of being as well as the first principle of knowledge.

At the same time, the mind arrives at this recognition of absolute equality through the analysis of sensible equality. It is sensible equality that prompts reflection into its own intelligible principle, namely, absolute equality. After all, human beings sense before they develop reasoning and reflection. However, this connection to absolute equality (and other forms) shows the deeper nature of the mind, namely, that the ultimate principles of knowledge are not derived, strictly speaking, from the sensible world. The soul, in having some connection to a changeless intelligible realm, is in some sense divinely ordered.

To Plato, the soul's connection with the eternal realm means that the soul is also eternal, having existed before its life in the body and being indestructible by physical death.[33] For the soul's knowledge of the forms must preexist its life in the body, since this knowledge is not derived, properly speaking, from the sensible world. The senses only provide the occasion for the soul to reflect on the invisible principles that ground its own knowledge. The senses only remind the soul of the forms, as Plato puts it; but the senses are not sufficient for the knowledge of the forms. What the soul remembers, namely, the forms, was not encountered in this life; the soul must have encountered what it now remembers prior to this life. At which point prior to this life? What the soul remembers are eternal principles. Can one remember eternal principles without having, in some sense, always known them? A definitive answer to this question may be impossible to demonstrate, but the more likely case is that the soul has always known these eternal principles, that the element by which the soul has a connection to these eternal principles is itself eternal. Accordingly, this divine element of the soul will also, in all likelihood, persist after the death of the body. However, what is undeniable is that the soul, insofar as it judges the sensible world in reference to the forms, possesses a vital connection to these forms, as well as a natural desire to know the forms as much as possible. The soul wants complete goodness, complete beauty, etc. The greatest fulfillment of the soul lies in truth and being, and the forms are the principles of truth and being.

33. See *Phaedo* 105d–107d. Plato argues for the soul's immortality in other places, such as *Republic* 608d–611a and *Phaedrus* 245c–246a.

The soul, ultimately, draws its vision from the Good, but its vision is really its substance, since the soul is a thinking substance that seeks knowledge by its very nature. However, the Good, the transcendent source and end of the soul, is not fully accessible to the incarnate soul, whose vision is clouded not only by the sensible world but also by the many necessities, passions, and distractions of the body. The human soul, intimately tied to its body from birth and habituated to relate to sensible objects the majority of the time, finds it extremely difficult to contemplate what is invisible and unchanging. When it does contemplate such objects, it can do so only incompletely and for a limited amount of time. Hence, the incarnate soul remains restless, since its natural bond to the divine forms cannot be fully consummated in this life. The soul itself, therefore, as seeker of its natural destination and origin, is this subsistent drive towards the goal that is also its source. Moreover, this goal and source is the very principle that preserves the being of the soul, as well as its vision. The human soul's very subsistence, therefore, is its love of wisdom. This love is grounded in its (presently weak) connection to the forms, so that this love both draws and directs its vital force towards the divine. The ultimate significance of the being of the soul is expressed through its love of wisdom.

I.2b
The Continuity and Confusion of Love

There is continuity between the sensible and intelligible worlds, since the sensible world shares in the intelligible world; the sensible world receives some being (that is, becoming) from the intelligible world. Similarly, the human being is a microcosm that reflects and relates to both dimensions. The human being both senses and thinks, and can therefore discover the deeper meaning of the sensible world, that it is a reflection of intelligible reality. However, of all the forms, beauty is most significant for the human experience, insofar as it provides for the soul the most powerful experience of continuity between sense and intelligence. Specifically, it is the basic attraction of the soul for beauty that moves the soul from the sensible to the intelligible realm. And the closest and most moving beauty is that which the human soul finds in another human being, the object of erotic love. This fundamental love for beauty is a fundamental love of wisdom, since beauty is the aspect of the Good (the cause of being and knowledge) that is most stimulating to the human soul.

Erotic love can be such a powerful experience because the human soul recognizes in the beloved a clear and intimate sign of Beauty itself.[34] At first, the soul is drawn intensely to the beloved in order to consummate its desire for possession and union. At the same time, in recognizing Beauty itself through the beloved, the soul's initial undivided resolve towards the beloved is sharply checked, for the soul discovers through and in the beloved an object of infinite respect, since the beloved reflects the Good. The fear of debasing the divine through sheer possession and subjection—that awesome fear that arises when coming close to unwittingly committing sacrilege—violently pulls the soul back from its initial instinctive drive. The soul is thrown into confusion (divine madness, as Plato puts it), since the powerful desire to possess the beloved is merged, in the experience of the lover, with the recognition of the ultimate divine principle. The powerful continuity between the sensible and intelligible, occasioned by erotic love, also shatters the human soul, which at once is drawn to the sensible as well as to the intelligible. Naturally, the relative influence of these dimensions upon a given soul depends on the inner order of the soul itself, upon its relative virtue. A vicious soul, dominated by instinct and appetite, will not feel the restraint of intellect and respect, will not understand that the power of Eros is ultimately love of wisdom, love of Beauty itself. Only the virtuous soul will be able to order these divergent drives into one and to create with its beloved a love that will contribute to the virtue of both, a love that brings them closer to the soul's ultimate fulfillment, namely, a love of wisdom. For only the virtuous soul truly lives by reason and truth.

I.2c
The Order of the Soul[35]

The complexity of the experience of love indicates the complexity of the soul itself, as well the type of unity necessary for the soul's virtue and happiness. The human soul has three parts—reason, spirit, and appetite. Reason is the part that understands and seeks knowledge. Spirit is the driving force of the soul, as well as the seat of the emotions. Appetite is the part associated with all the needs, desires, and urges of the body. These three parts are discovered through the soul's inner conflicts. For if the soul desires different

---

34. *Phaedrus* 250b–256e.

35. The parts and order of the soul are best described in *Republic* 435c–445b. This section and the next rely on this text primarily.

things at the same time, this can be only through different parts of itself, since no thing both wants and does not want the same thing, at the same time, and in the same respect. For example, the soul may desire to eat a given food, yet it restrains itself because it knows that the food is unhealthy. Two parts of the soul are at play here, namely, reason and appetite. To give another example, the soul may be dominated by anger and act violently, even though the soul knew that patience was necessary. This case indicates the difference between reason and spirit. Spirit and appetite may also conflict, as when the fear of punishment restrains someone wishing to steal.

Even though the soul is capable of many different kinds of appetite, emotion, and knowledge, there are only three parts of the soul, for two reasons. First, the principles that rule the soul's choices always fall into the categories of reason, spirit, and appetite. Second, the resolution of the soul's inner conflicts is always among these three parts, and not within any one of these three parts. For an appetite, purely on its own account, does not restrain another appetite, and an emotion, purely on its own account, does not restrain another emotion. If the soul has two appetites that cannot be fulfilled at a given time, the soul chooses to fulfill one instead of the other, because of either reason or emotion (or both working together). For, in this case, the soul actually desires to fulfill both appetites; the choice of one over the other stems from another principle. If the soul experiences divergent emotions, such as fear and anger, that push it to different courses of action, the soul will choose a given course of action, because of either reason or appetite (or both working together).

In terms of commanding the soul, reason, spirit, and appetite have natural aptitudes. Reason is by nature meant to rule the soul, since reason can direct the soul through the knowledge of what is best for the soul. Reason recognizes (or at least can learn to recognize) what is true and false, what is good and bad. Moreover, reason is able to assess, judge, and advise the emotions as well as the appetites, in order to approve some of them and subdue others, for the sake of what is best for the whole soul. On the other hand, the emotions, of themselves, do not possess understanding and so are not able to guide the soul as well as reason can. However, spirit does recognize the dictates of reason as well as the influence of the appetites. For example, the spirit may feel shame when it recognizes failure or anger when it feels hunger. On the other hand, the appetites of themselves have no share in understanding at all, nor do they experience the other parts of the soul. The appetites, therefore, because of their natural aptitude, should have no commanding role in the soul. Rather, they are meant to be ruled by the rest of the soul.

Unlike the appetites, spirit does have the natural aptitude to participate in the government of the soul. For the spirit is a natural ally of reason. The spirit always feels shame when it fails to follow what reason knows is right, and always feels pride when it endures and overcomes for the sake of reason. Thus, whenever there is a conflict between reason and appetite, spirit in a sense always allies itself with reason, since even though spirit may on a given occasion drive the soul towards the fulfillment of an appetite that reason disapproves, spirit will feel shame to have let the appetite win over reason. For spirit always recognizes the superiority of reason, even when it does not follow reason. Naturally, even though reason is the soul's best resource, it may happen that reason is wrong about what is best, in a given circumstance. For example, reason may think that a given food is unhealthy but later discover that the food is not only healthy but also necessary. What is significant, however, is that spirit always allies itself with reason's conviction. Accordingly, the spirit, the part that fights for the sake of the whole soul, has the natural aptitude to obey and help reason, to enact the dictates of reason. After all, knowing what course of action is best is not sufficient for the actual choice of this course of action. In order for reason to accomplish a goal and, more generally, a certain way of life, the assistance of spirit is essential.

Even though each of the three parts of the soul has a natural aptitude—reason is meant to rule, spirit is meant to assist reason, and the appetites are meant to be ruled by reason and its assistant (spirit)—the soul's parts may fail to accomplish the roles for which they are naturally suited. For example, a given soul may be ruled by certain appetites, whereby the soul's reason occupies itself in planning how to satisfy these appetites, and the soul's spirit fights and endures for the sake of satisfying them. Or, a soul may be ruled by certain dimensions of the spirit—pride, for instance—whereby the soul's reason works for the satisfaction of pride, and the soul's appetites are either subdued or approved for the sake of pride.

In other words, the principle that rules in a given soul is the principle for the sake of which the other principles of the soul work. Moreover, the three parts of the soul are always present in human life. The rule of one part over another never implies the total absence of the latter, since thought, emotion, and appetite are always part of human experience, in some way. In fact, living well is the harmony among these parts, whereby the three parts are satisfied in performing the roles for which they have a natural aptitude. It is vice, rather, that entails the unhappy subjugation of some parts by others, precisely because vice exists when the parts of the soul perform roles for which they have no natural aptitude. Accordingly, the proper order among these parts is essential, not only for virtue but also for happiness. In fact, virtue is happiness (as Socrates would also say), since virtue is the best condition for the soul, and the soul is fulfilled only when it is in an excellent condition.

I.2d
Virtue as Unity and as a Way of Life

In establishing that the parts of the soul are meant to perform certain roles rather than others because they have the natural ability to perform these roles rather than others, Plato also establishes that the soul has a natural aptitude for virtue. The soul is meant to be virtuous, even though it is also capable of vice. For the virtuous soul is the one in which the three parts actually perform the roles for which they have a natural aptitude. The excellent soul is the soul that develops its natural aptitude in the proper way. The soul that guides its life on the basis of what reason knows to be best possesses wisdom, not in an absolute sense, but in the sense that this soul cultivates and lives by reason. However, in order for the soul to live by reason, it must have courage: spirit must fight and endure for the sake of what reason knows to be best. Otherwise, the soul could not live by reason, since reason, purely through the possession of knowledge, is not sufficient for the enactment of what it knows to be best. Moreover, without courage so defined, reason could not commit itself to the philosophical way of life, to the consistent pursuit of truth.

The wise soul needs not only courage but also temperance, namely, the control of the appetites by reason and spirit. Temperance is not the total suppression of the appetites. After all, the human being has many necessary appetites, such as those relating to food, clothing, and shelter. Rather, temperance is the moderation and regulation of the appetites, which satisfies them without strengthening them to the point that they sway the soul. If the basic physical needs of the soul are not fulfilled, the soul is always preoccupied with its survival and security; reason is not free, in this case, but rather enslaved by the needs of the body. On the other hand, if the appetites are indulged to the point that they multiply into unnecessary and unlimited urges and cravings, they have grown to the point that they contend with reason and spirit, precisely because now reason must think about how to satisfy them, and spirit strives to do so. Temperance is the state whereby the appetites can be and are satisfied with what is truly necessary, the state that rejects both the insufficient and the excessive.[36] If temperate, the appetites are happy to be ruled by reason and (its assistant) spirit; they are contented and, most importantly, reason and spirit are freed to pursue their respective natural callings, namely, the application, pursuit, and cultivation of knowledge. A soul that subdues strong appetites in order to do what reason deems best is to be commended, but a soul that finds pleasure in following reason because its appetites are well regulated is to be commended even more. Moreover, in the strict sense, only the latter soul is temperate, for only the latter soul is genuinely self-controlled, since there is less chance of subversion within the soul.

When reason, spirit, and appetite do what they are meant to do in terms of the government of the soul, there is virtue in the soul—wisdom, courage, temperance, as well as justice. For justice is virtue in the complete sense. Justice means that all the parts of the soul are performing at their best because they are performing the roles for which they have a natural aptitude, not roles for which they are ill-suited. Wisdom and courage are virtues of specific parts of the soul, namely, reason and spirit respectively. Temperance and justice, on the other hand, involve the whole soul. Temperance is the peaceful agreement between those who rule (reason and spirit) and those who are ruled (appetites). Justice, on the other hand, is the excellence of the three parts, whereby the three parts answer to their natural callings and thereby contribute the excellence that only they can contribute. When each part of the soul is excellent, the whole soul is excellent. In this sense, justice is virtue or excellence in the complete sense.

Since justice is complete excellence, justice is the harmony, happiness, and strength ("health") of the soul. As noted, that each part of the soul has a natural aptitude implies that the whole soul has a natural aptitude, namely, an aptitude for virtue (justice). This natural aptitude for virtue is also a natural aptitude for unity (harmony) and happiness, since reason should

---

36. Plato favors the mean in virtue. See *Republic* 619b. Also, when speaking about justice in the ideal city, he indicates how the extremes of wealth and poverty corrupt the class of craftsmen (ibid., 421c–d). In his analogy between the classes of the city and the parts of the soul, the craftsmen correspond to the appetites, which are similarly corrupted by excess and deficiency. This preference for the mean will be central in Aristotle's ethical theory.

rule, spirit should assist the ruler, and appetite should be ruled. If these parts actually do what they should do in the government of the soul, each part finds true fulfillment in excelling at its natural calling, and the whole soul is at peace. No part interferes or conflicts with another, and the soul is genuinely harmonious and one. This soul is truly strong or healthy, since it has unity of action, purpose, and conscience. The just soul listens to reason, has the strength to follow reason, and finds pleasure in following reason. The whole soul is at peace, in harmony, and finds happiness in living in the best possible way according to its nature. Virtue, unity, strength, and happiness indicate the same reality in the soul.

Naturally, virtue is always a work in progress (as Socrates would also say) and never a fixed and immutable state. For human life is an active process that requires the cultivation and pursuit of wisdom, courage, temperance, and justice. It is always possible for a given soul to move either away from or toward virtue, depending on the choices it makes in the circumstances it faces. For, regarding virtue and vice, the soul becomes what it does; virtuous activity strengthens virtue, and vicious activity weakens it. Nevertheless virtue is more stable than vice, since unity is more stable than disunity. The more virtuous a soul is, the stronger is its tendency to remain in the one state in which it is meant to be.

The soul possesses unity and happiness to the extent that it possesses justice. The more a soul pursues wisdom through reason, implements in life what it knows to be best through the spirit, and finds pleasure in the rule of reason through well-regulated appetites, the more unified and contented this soul is. On the other hand, the more a soul falls away from this ideal, the more divided and wretched it is. A soul dominated by appetites eventually acts against what reason knows to be best for the whole soul, like a man who harms his health by indulging a vice or betrays friends because of monetary ambition. The soul of this man is divided, since the part of him that should rule knows (in the desolate place that vice has relegated to it) that health should be sought, or that he should be true to his friends. Yet, his appetites are so strong that his spirit serves these appetites rather than reason, fighting and enduring for them at the expense of reason. Inevitably, inner conflict and regret are present in this soul. Similarly, a soul dominated by spirit eventually acts against what reason knows to be best for the whole soul, like the man who is so proud that he refuses to accept and learn from his mistakes. Inevitably, this man harms himself and others he cares about, and feels regret in the process, since the part of him that should rule knows (in the desolate place that vice has relegated to it) that it is best to accept and learn from one's mistakes. For the pursuit of wisdom requires humility, and only this pursuit equips the soul to make the best possible decisions.

Strictly speaking, therefore, one or more virtues cannot exist without the rest of the virtues. Wisdom requires courage, temperance, and justice. Courage requires wisdom, since genuine courage is the enforcement of what reason knows is best, as well as temperance, since without temperance the soul lives not by reason but by appetite. Hence, courage also requires justice, since justice means that reason, spirit, and appetite are doing what they are meant to do. Temperance requires wisdom, since wisdom determines which appetites need to be satisfied and in which way, and which appetites need to be reduced or eliminated for the good of the whole soul. Temperance also requires courage, since this knowledge about the best state of the appetites needs to be applied consistently in life. Strength of will is therefore necessary. In requiring courage and wisdom, temperance also requires justice, by definition. Finally, justice includes wisdom, courage, and temperance, since justice is the proper order of the soul, whereby each part of the soul functions excellently, whereby there is virtue in the complete sense. To repeat, one virtue cannot exist without the others, even though virtue always needs practice, and always admits of improvement.

However, to the extent that vice takes over the soul, to that extent is reason silenced as a ruling principle, since the vicious soul uses and exercises reason only as a slave of the spirit or appetites (or both). Yet wretchedness and inner conflict provide some indication to the vicious soul that its condition is not as it should be, even though this may not be sufficient for real change. After all, the vicious soul is the soul that finds pleasure in the wrong things, even when this harms the soul as a whole. Real change towards virtue implies change in the soul's likes and dislikes; for the vicious soul to become virtuous, it must learn to enjoy the rule of reason with the assistance of spirit, as well as the moderate pleasures that support this rule. This soul must learn to love living the life for which it has a natural aptitude, the life and condition that is proper to it. In a word, this soul must learn to love wisdom with its whole being.

Virtue, in the complete sense, is justice, not only within the soul but also in a political sense. First, the just soul will not encroach upon others, since it is not dominated by either emotions or appetites. This soul, more than any other, is capable of respecting others and their rights, of understanding and following good laws. For this soul recognizes that good conduct depends on principles that are true for any human soul. Hence this soul, more than any other, is capable of abiding by the same principles that apply to others. Reason also recognizes that the good of the community as a whole is greater and more important than any private good, and that this greater good depends upon laws that ensure peace and order and that contribute to the development and preservation of virtue.

A just city is peaceful and unified, like a just soul. What ensures peace and unity is the rule of reason, which in the individual considers and implements what is best for the soul as a whole, with the approval of the whole soul, and in the city considers and implements what is best for the city as a whole, with the approval of the whole city. The just city is also like the just soul, since it is based on the principle of excellence. The truly just city is the city that identifies and develops the different natural talents and aptitudes of its citizens. For in this city, the citizens find fulfillment in excelling according to their individual talents and benefit the city as a whole in providing the city with the best that the citizens can provide. On the other hand, cities where individuals engage in activities for which they have no capacity breed ineptitude and injustice, especially when the rulers are not qualified to rule, since the city fosters patterns that are harmful to itself and its citizens. Finally, a just city, like a just soul, is strong when it possesses unity, when there is no inner conflict or civil war, while unjust souls and cities are divided and therefore weak.

Hence Plato's analogy between the soul and the city is extremely fertile and is the central theme of his greatest work, *The Republic*. However, insofar as the classes of Plato's city (guardians, auxiliaries, and craftsmen) correspond to the parts of the soul (reason, spirit, and appetite), this analogy should be interpreted with care, since it cannot be taken completely literally. For, since every soul has three parts, and every soul is capable of virtue in the complete sense, Plato cannot be propounding that the virtuous city is one in which the citizens cultivate only a given aspect of the soul, when he connects reason to the guardians, spirit to the auxiliaries, and appetites to the craftsmen. In other words, if one uses *The Republic* as evidence for Plato's position as to the best form of government for actual societies, the connection between political classes and parts of the soul cannot be taken in an exclusive or absolute sense, and Plato indicates as much.[37] Engaging in this interpretation, however, is not the present purpose.

---

37. See ibid., 443d–e.

I.2e
The Soul as Lover[38]

What is clear is that for Plato justice, as complete virtue, is the best condi-tion for the soul, as well as the basis for just social relations. This is sufficient to see not only the political significance of Plato's account of justice but also the significance of love of wisdom in his account. The soul's virtue entails the proper order and unification of its faculties, whereby the soul obtains genuine freedom and fulfillment in the cultivation of reason, in the pursuit of wisdom. In other words, love of wisdom indicates the freest and the most fulfilling life for the whole soul.

The soul, according to Plato, is a lover. Fundamentally, the soul is a lover of wisdom, since reason, the commanding faculty of the soul, seeks the truth, which is grounded in being. Truth and being satisfy because they are complete and permanent. Appearance and becoming, on the other hand, are dependent and diminished states. Truth and being are found in the intelligible forms, with which the soul has a basic connection, since the forms sustain the soul's vision and knowledge. Only intelligible reality, ultimately the Good, is capable of fulfilling the soul's nature. However, the soul is more than simply reason. In order for reason to approach intelli-gible reality, reason needs the strength of spirit, since a life committed to the pursuit of wisdom entails exertion, consistency, and will. Plato calls the spirit a lover of honor, since the spirit's proper satisfaction consists in the recognition that it has performed its duty well, that it has obeyed and sup-ported reason. Insofar as the soul is driven towards true reality, insofar as the soul actively pursues the divine, reason relies on spirit, its natural ally.

Finally, the incarnate soul also includes appetites, due to the many needs and desires of the body. In this life, as noted, reason and spirit should regulate these appetites in order for the soul to live well. However, the im-mortal or divine aspect of the soul does not include the appetites, which are identified with bodily life, even though the appetites may influence and even dominate the immortal aspect. The immortal soul's natural de-sire for true reality may be misdirected by the soul, if the soul learns to love material reality too much and so confuses it with true reality. This is precisely what happens to the soul dominated by appetites. However,

38. Plato describes the parts of the soul in terms of their corresponding loves, in ibid., 580e–581e.

the rule of the appetites only multiplies and strengthens them.[39] The more that the appetites are stimulated and multiplied, the more difficult it is to satisfy them, and the less that the higher aspects of the soul—reason and spirit—are fulfilled. The immortal soul's natural desire for true reality may be likewise misdirected if the spirit dominates the soul, if the soul comes to seek honor, recognition and power above all things. This soul comes to believe that true reality is honor and power over others, things that are ultimately dependent on others, and the more it thrives in these things, the more it comes to believe that only they matter. This soul, therefore, is not able to reach true satisfaction, since it only gratifies one aspect of itself at the expense of others.

Only the soul that is a lover of wisdom, with its whole self, can approach true excellence and fulfillment. In fact, the soul that is a genuine lover of wisdom—a lover of true reality—must unify and thereby strengthen its being. In other words, this soul must develop itself so that it becomes as close in nature to the reality it desires. This soul must become truly one and rational; only in this condition is the soul prepared for communion with the corresponding unity and intelligibility of true being. In other words, love of wisdom is both a drive towards a goal as well as a self-transformation; the very pursuit demands growth in virtue, as Socrates would also say. For Plato, as for Socrates, the genuine pursuit of philosophy is not merely theoretical, but also practical. Moreover, the philosophical pursuit is identified with the best way to seek happiness, as well as with the highest form of human freedom.

Virtue, freedom, and happiness are also identified in Aristotle's version of love of wisdom. Much of Plato remains in the philosophy of his student Aristotle. However, Aristotle also develops love of wisdom in an original way. Aristotelian love of wisdom interprets and grounds itself on new principles, giving a whole new meaning to this core human drive. It is to Aristotle's own love of wisdom that we now turn.

I.3
ARISTOTLE'S LOVE OF WISDOM:
DESIRE FOR ACTUALIZATION ACCORDING TO FORM

Plato's philosophy, like Socrates', grounds itself on the soul's self-examination, which shows the soul its true nature and ultimate goal. As noted,

39. See *Phaedo* 83b–d.

Plato develops this Socratic focus in original ways. Plato's love of wisdom originates in the soul's experience of itself as grounded in divine, intelligible being, and so this love directs itself primarily towards the intelligible realm, and interprets its experience in the world of becoming as a sign of true being, as a ladder towards true being. For Plato, becoming is not fully knowable; becoming is the object of opinion, not knowledge. Becoming is a copy that is meant to point the soul in the direction of what it represents—intelligible reality. To Plato, philosophy begins by reflecting on becoming, since becoming is what first reminds the soul of true being. However, to Plato, becoming is a reference to being, and ultimately not knowable on its own terms. To Aristotle, on the other hand, love of wisdom is fundamentally rooted in becoming itself, in the following sense.

I.3a
The Desire to Know

Aristotle's love of wisdom originates in a fundamental desire to understand what we observe in our world of growth, change, sense and process, in the rich sphere of our human experience. This world not only surrounds and contains us. We grow out of this world. We are its children. This rootedness in the world we experience draws us to understand it, and implies a fundamental kinship between us as seekers of knowledge and what is knowable in our world. To Aristotle, our world of sense and change, the world of becoming that Plato did not consider fully knowable, fuels the original drive for wisdom and is the proper focus of philosophical investigation. From this investigation Aristotle does gather evidence about beings and causes that transcend the world of human experience. However, Aristotle comes to understand transcendent beings and causes in reference to becoming, namely, as principles and causes of becoming.

Aristotle develops the fundamental kinship between the human being and the sensible world in *De Anima* (*On the Soul*), where he discusses the various levels of life and cognition.[40] In the *Metaphysics*, he suggests this kinship in the very first line, where he states, "All human beings by nature desire to know." He gives evidence for this claim by pointing out that the pleasures of sensation indicate human nature's inherent desire to

---

40. For Aristotle, the human soul adequately communicates at various levels with all existing things, whether sensible or intelligible. He summarizes this general conception in *De Anima* 3.8.431b20–432a2.

know. Pleasure is central in human experience, since human beings pursue pleasure for its own sake.[41] When we enjoy an activity, the activity is truly meaningful, since it possesses an intrinsic purpose. Without pleasure, on the other hand, the activity is merely instrumental, since it is done for an end other than itself. In pointing to the inherent pleasures of sensation (such as seeing beautiful sights, tasting, etc.), Aristotle indicates that human life shares a basic bond with the sensible world and that this bond manifests itself at the most basic level of cognition. For the senses and their information are for human nature pleasant and worthy in themselves. The pleasures of sensation show that human beings value knowledge for its own sake already at this first level of knowledge. Even though sensation is only the most elementary level of knowledge, the development of knowledge will not leave the sensible world behind. On the contrary, knowledge improves insofar as it can reach a more comprehensive grasp of the patterns and causes of this world. Moreover, sensation, as the first origin of knowledge, contains in raw form the vital pulse of the human desire for knowledge: cognition is pleasant, worthy in itself.

After sensation, memory is the next step in the ladder of knowledge.[42] With memory, sense information can be retained and preserved for future reference. Without memory, that which is sensed would be known only while sensed, only immediately. Only animals with memory can learn, since only they retain what they have sensed and therefore can use what they remember when they sense something similar in the future. The sensible world becomes accessible in a more comprehensive way through memory. Experience provides an even more comprehensive perspective, since experience judges memories. Through experience, we know that some things are connected with other things, even though we may not know the cause of the connection, even though we may lack the knowledge proper to art. As Aristotle illustrates, we may know through experience that a certain medicine is beneficial in some circumstances, but only the doctor knows which class of people qualifies for the medicine, as well as the dosage that is proper in each case. In other words, only the doctor knows the causal relation between the medicine and the patient in a universal way, so that only the doctor prescribes medicine by applying general principles to many individual cases. That is why, in some circumstances, only doctors can and

41. See his discussion in *Nicomachean Ethics* 10.4–5.

42. Aristotle describes the different levels of knowledge, from sense perception to wisdom, in *Metaphysics* 1.1–2.

should prescribe. Art, therefore, in establishing causal connections, provides an even more comprehensive perspective of our world than mere experience, memory, and sense.

Arts such as building and agriculture, Aristotle notes, emerged in order to satisfy certain necessities, in this case shelter and food. Once a society begins to satisfy basic needs, arts that aim at giving pleasure—what we would call fine arts, such as drama and music—can begin to emerge. These arts are nobler, since their true origin is the human desire for enjoyment, for activities that are fulfilling in themselves. These arts are nobler, precisely because their essence is not utilitarian or servile, even though some individuals might pursue these arts purely for money or other utilitarian purposes (the effect this has on fine art is another question). However, art (servile or fine) is not the highest knowledge, since art is fundamentally know-how (*techne*), namely, knowledge ordered to production or performance. As such, art does not aim exclusively at knowledge for its own sake.

On the other hand, science, as understood by Aristotle, does. The different sciences investigate reality for the very purpose of knowing reality. They investigate the being of their different subject matters: biology investigates being as living, anthropology investigates human being, etc. A science attains knowledge when it demonstrates the properties of its subject through the causes of the subject,[43] as when geometry demonstrates properties of figures through certain axioms and definitions. However, the perspective of these sciences is still limited, since they concern themselves only with the being that they have demarked for themselves. Even though science seeks knowledge for its own sake, science is not the highest form of knowledge, since science does not consider reality in its fullness, or in the most comprehensive way. Science is not wisdom. Wisdom investigates what is most real or knowable, namely, the principles and causes that govern being as such. These are the first principles and causes, by which everything ultimately is and is known.[44]

These first principles and causes are most real or knowable not in the sense that they are easiest to learn but in the sense that, as first, they are the ground of everything else.[45] However, they are last in the order of human learning, which begins with sensation and increases as it backs away from immediate sensation in order to gain a more comprehensive or universal

---

43. See *Posterior Analytics* 1.2.71b8–12.

44. *Metaphysics* 4.1.1003a21–28.

45. Ibid., 1.2.982a28–b3.

perspective of our world. Wisdom, therefore, is the knowledge that is most removed from the senses. At the same time, wisdom provides the best knowledge of the universe, since it considers everything in light of what is first. Wisdom is the highest knowledge as well as the freest, since this knowledge above all is pursued for its own sake and, accordingly, seeks what is most knowable. Moreover, wisdom is the most pleasant form of knowledge, since it fulfills the basic human desire to know in the fullest sense. However, for these same reasons—for being freest, best, and concerned with first causes—wisdom belongs to divine being more than to human beings. Wisdom, strictly speaking, is the knowledge that God possesses, since God is the first, eternal cause of the universe. Human beings, who are mortal, needy, and servile in many ways, may be called wise only with serious qualifications.[46]

This fact, however, should not encourage us to focus only on the lowly and mortal. On the contrary, human beings should be lovers of wisdom as much as their natures allow, since wisdom (in any measure possible) is the ultimate and most fulfilling goal of human beings, who by nature desire to know. Moreover, human beings can satisfy their desire to know by discovering causes of the world they experience. Human beings might not be capable of understanding all of these causes adequately or in themselves, especially not those divine causes that transcend us. However, basic causes may be gathered through an analysis of the phenomena accessible to us. The analysis of change, the first focus of philosophical questioning, ultimately leads to the first principles and causes proper to wisdom.

I.3b
The Basic Question

Aristotle's *Physics* deals with nature and becoming in the broadest sense. In this work, he lays out fundamental principles of his philosophy, later applied in more specific areas, such as psychology. After all, the human soul or life principle is part of nature, even though it does include a divine element (as shall be shown). Accordingly, fundamental principles of natural philosophy may also be applied (with the requisite adjustments) to the question of human happiness, as one may discover in the *Nicomachean Ethics*. Even in his *Metaphysics*, where he deals with the last and highest achievement of human knowledge (wisdom), he begins by considering the

46. Ibid., 982b28–983a11.

causes and principles considered in the *Physics*.[47] Even though Aristotle agrees with Socrates and Plato in holding that the highest truths are divine and thus beyond the full human grasp, in understanding philosophy as love of wisdom rather than as wisdom simply, for Aristotle there is a genuine sense in which human beings may be called wise in terms of the possession of wisdom. For even though the first causes of the universe ultimately transcend the human intellect, philosophy's original and fundamental drive—to understand the world from which we spring, on its own terms—may be satisfied in significant ways.

Becoming, as Plato would also say, depends ultimately on unchanging being. Unlike Plato, and as mentioned earlier, Aristotle approaches becoming on its own terms because for him it must be knowable on its own terms. The reason, however, is not the well-known fact that Aristotle places the forms of things in the individual things we experience. The reason must be more basic. For Aristotle arrives at his position that the forms are in things from his consideration of becoming. In other words, Aristotle's philosophical investigation is based on a prior and more fundamental intuition. This intuition is twofold. On the one hand, human beings, children of the world of growth and change, are equipped to know the world in which they are rooted. On the other hand, self-evident facts, such as the fact that some things change, are principles of knowledge and action, and should be approached accordingly. Hence, when we cannot explain fully what is self-evident, we must not deny its reality but rather seek its causes.

In terms of philosophical focus, Aristotle is not original but part of a long tradition of natural philosophy beginning with Thales of Miletus, who lived in the late seventh and early sixth centuries BC. In fact, for Aristotle, the history of previous philosophy has been a series of attempts to understand the nature of change.[48] These previous attempts have been ultimately unsatisfactory, but there have been advances and even mistakes from which one may learn in order to reach the truth.

The original philosophical question, Aristotle tells us, the question that elicited wonder in his predecessors and drove them to philosophize, concerns the nature of things that change and grow, things that come into being and pass away. In particular, the question concerns the reality of new being. Does something new come into being, and if so, how? Moreover, since passing away seems to result in a new condition, in a condition that

---

47. Ibid., 1.3.983a24–b1.

48. See ibid., 1.3–5.

did not exist before, the question pertains to passing away as well. In our world of change and growth, new beings and new states seem evident: new babies are born, new trees grow, new colors emerge, etc. What is new, insofar as it is new, did not exist at some point in the past. So, where does that which is new, insofar as it is new, come from? For if that which is new already existed before in a different way, it is not really new. On the other hand, if that which is new is new in an absolute sense, and does not preexist in any sense, then we are forced to say that what is new as such comes from nothing. Either case is problematic, but the latter case is more problematic.

The first case, namely, that new things are not really new because they preexist somehow, is problematic because it goes against our experience. The newborn who recently joined our home seems truly new. Sure, she comes from the parents, but she also is a unique individual, and this unique individuality, which seems very new and very real, does not seem likely to have preexisted at any point in the past. Our experience of her novelty is so strong that we do treat her as a unique individual, and the more she grows, the more unique she becomes, and the greater the novelty she brings into our lives. The second case—namely, that what is new, insofar as it is new, is both real and did not exist at all before, therefore it comes from nothing— commits violence to reason. "From nothing, nothing comes" is reputedly the first axiom in the history of philosophy, and is also logically necessary. This second option is inadmissible.

Accordingly, since the first philosophers approached the question of coming to be and ceasing to be by maintaining that new phenomena preexist somehow, philosophy began by submitting sense experience to reason. What sense experience conveys in strong terms, namely, the genuine reality of what is new, must be only apparent, not real. After all, sense experience is often deceiving, precisely because what appears need not be the case. For these first philosophers, new being cannot be a genuine emergence into being or a genuine passing away from being. Rather, changes must be dependent upon that which does not change, that which does not enter into being or fall away from being. True being, therefore, must be eternal and unchanging. This is apprehended by reason: since nothing comes from nothing, every change presupposes a principle that persists. On the other hand, the senses, insofar as they apprehend changing reality, do not apprehend true being. Moreover, true being must be one. Since this principle underlies every change and itself does not admit of change, it always retains its identity and remains what it is. Hence the first principle—being—is one, not many.

Accordingly, the first philosophers were monists. However, although they agreed as to the eternity, unity, and immutability of the first principle, they differed in terms of their understanding of the first principle itself. Some, such as Thales and Anaximenes, understood this principle as a principle in motion. Thales posited that water was the underlying principle of all things and that all things are modifications of water, while Anaximenes posited air. Others, such as Parmenides and his follower Melissus, understood this principle as a motionless principle. For Parmenides and Melissus, being itself or the One is completely at rest and in no way related to change. For being simply is and there is no sense in which it is not. Hence, being admits of no modifications or differences (since every modification or difference would be other than being itself, and to be other than being is to be what is not). Hence, being is purely self-identical, one and, therefore, completely at rest. Parmenides was the first for whom change was simply illusory as completely cut off from being, which is accessible only to reason.[49]

To Aristotle, these thinkers began by trying to explain change, but they ended up explaining it away. For in positing a principle that persists in every change, these monists actually explained that which does not change, not that which changes insofar as it changes. The novelty of change, which is central to our experience, has not been accounted for through only one principle. If being is only one principle, then the plurality, variety, and novelty that we experience are not true reality. This is true whether the first principle is in motion (like Thales' water) or at rest (like Parmenides' One). Similarly, to Aristotle, Plato's forms fail to explain change. For these forms are not subject to motion or connected to motion, since they are separate from changing things. How can changeless, separate principles act upon the changing things that we experience? To Aristotle, to say that changing things participate in the changeless forms is to use empty words, since this description does not convey how change actually occurs.[50]

At the same time, the monists did contribute toward the explanation of change. For it stands to reason that every change implies something that persists, something that remains and does not change. Otherwise, change would be the emergence of something absolutely new, of something out

---

49. This position of Parmenides was very influential in Plato and in the history of philosophy in general.

50. See *Metaphysics* 1.9.

of nothing, which is inconceivable. However, the monists did not go far enough in their explanation. The next significant advance came with thinkers who posited contraries in order to explain change.[51] For example, Empedocles posited the contrary principles of Love and Strife in order to make sense of natural cycles. Others posited different contraries, such as hot and cold, dry and wet. These thinkers, insofar as they posited contraries, did see something fundamental: change always involves some type of contrariety, since nothing can exist actually in two contrary conditions at the same time. When a thing changes, the new state that the thing assumes by definition excludes the old state that it no longer possesses. However, insofar as these thinkers posited only contraries as their principles of change, they fell short. For contraries, as contraries, cannot act on each other. Pure heat, for example, cannot influence pure cold. A third principle that mediates between the contraries is necessary in order for heat to influence cold, as when water goes from a cold to a hot state. In this case, water mediates the contrary states, and itself goes from one contrary state to the other.

I.3c
Change, Form, and Actualization

Aristotle's explanation of change is in a way a synthesis between the monists and the dualists, even though he does conceive of nature in terms of different forms, unlike these thinkers.[52] Every change entails three principles, namely, the two contraries and the principle that persists in the change. This latter principle is always an underlying subject that can go from one contrary state to the other. This principle is capable of assuming both contrary states, but never simultaneously, since acquiring one contrary state by definition entails losing the other contrary state. For no thing can be both contraries at the same time. Water can be either hot or cold, but not hot and cold at the same time. When water acquires the quality of hot, water by definition loses the quality of cold. Hence change is always the movement by a subject from one condition to the contrary condition. Change is real, since the subject does not merely underlie or persist in the change (as in the monist theory); the subject also changes in a real way, although not in every way. Hence water that becomes hot after being cold does indeed change,

51. See *Physics* 1.5.

52. The core of his explanation, including his assessment of his predecessors, is found in ibid., 1.7–9.

since the water loses one contrary state in order to assume the other. However, the water does not change insofar as it is water. The water did persist and did underlie the change, while at the same time it did acquire a new condition, namely, the quality of hot.

Aristotle uses these three principles, namely, two contraries and one subject, in order to explain every type of change. In every type of change, one contrary gives way to the other, as the underlying subject (which is capable of both contraries) moves from one contrary to the other, while this subject also retains its identity as a subject. Every change, no matter how minute, is both real and explainable in terms of contrariety. For whatever new condition the subject acquires entails the absence of that which is not new. For example, when water only changes in temperature by one fraction of a degree, there is still a real change that entails the absence of what is newly acquired, since water cannot possess the new condition and the absence of the new condition at the same time. The contrary of the newly acquired temperature is not the negation of the new temperature, but rather the absence of the new temperature. For example, when water changes from 50 to 50.1 degrees the newly acquired temperature is 50.1 degrees. However, its contrary is not negative 50.1 degrees, but rather simply the absence of 50.1 degrees, since the presence of this temperature entails the loss of the absence of this temperature (whatever temperature the water might have had before the change). Accordingly, Aristotle always understands the contraries in terms of the newly acquired condition: the contraries are (1) the new condition, and (2) the privation or absence of this new condition. This is essential to convey the nature of change: change always entails something new that did not exist before, change always entails the persistence of some subject, and finally, change always affects the subject, not as subject, but in another respect.

Change is real, in the sense that new conditions are truly acquired by different subjects. Hence Aristotle classifies the different types of change according to patterns observed in nature. After all, since the changes we experience are real, we can base our understanding of nature on (careful) observation. Two chief types of change are evident. In one type of change, a subject acquires a new condition, as when a small dog grows and becomes a big dog. In another type of change, the dog comes into being or passes away. The first type of change affects a certain subject that is already in existence; the second type of change produces or destroys a given subject. Both types of change must be distinguished, because in one type of change the subject persists as subject while it changes in a certain respect. The dog remains a dog as it grows, yet the dog changes in terms of its size. In the other type of change, the subject does not persist, or, to put it in another way, the subject changes in an absolute way. For when the dog comes into being, the dog itself is the newly acquired reality, and when the dog passes away, the dead body of the dog is the newly acquired reality. This latter type of change, which is change without qualification, also presupposes a subject: some biological material, which can become the dog but is not the dog yet, actually becomes the dog through canine generation, and so this material acquires a new condition, namely, the condition of a living, individual dog. Both types of change still can be explained in terms of two contraries and one subject. However, these types of change are qualitatively different, since one type of change produces or destroys beings that themselves become the subjects for other changes.

In his account of change or motion[53]—subjects move from one contrary to another—Aristotle discovered potentiality and actuality, as well as the existence of forms in individual things. For change is the actualization of potency, and this actualization is the acquisition of form. Thus all change entails matter and form. The forms of things stem from the potency of material subjects; these forms are actual states acquired by potential matter. These forms may be either part of a subject or constitutive of a subject, depending on the type of change. For example, the dog that changes in size acquires a new form or state, namely, a new quantity. However, the new dog that is generated has received from its parents the very form by which it is a dog, its very life as a dog. In this latter sense, form is constitutive of a being, whether in nature or in art. This is the fundamental sense of form, which shall now be developed.

Form and matter function differently regarding natural and artificial beings, the two chief types of beings we experience. In natural things, form is the inherent principle governing the actualization and motion of matter.[54] Moreover, natural living things are generated from other living things

53. Motion should be taken here as a broad term that includes the various types of change. Motion refers not only to change of place (locomotion) but also includes change in quantity, change in quality, as well as coming into being and passing away.

54. See *Physics* 2.1. Natural things are further divided into living (e.g., plants) and nonliving (e.g., rocks). The former are characterized by having nutrition, growth, and reproduction, which the latter lack. But both possess form understood as an inherent principle of motion and actuality. In this section, we focus on natural living things, since this bears upon the human form and love of wisdom.

of the same form. Dogs generate dogs. The form of the dog is the principle by which the dog grows, acts, develops, and reproduces. In artificial things, on the other hand, the form is produced by an external agent of a different form. Thus, the craftsman works wood into a certain shape for a certain purpose. The matter and the form together make one being, such as a wooden tennis racket. In artificial things, the cause that produces (the craftsman), the formed matter (the racket), and the purpose (in this case, playing tennis) are causes that are quite independent of each other. The craftsman, a human being, is completely different from the racket, and the racket is distinct from its purpose, since the racket is still a racket even when it is not being used in a tennis game.

In living things, on the other hand, the producing cause is of the same form as the product; roses generate roses and pigeons pigeons. Moreover, a living thing, insofar as it is living, is always performing its function or purpose. This purpose is development and preservation according to form. Thus, seeds grow into full-blown trees that strive to endure. In living things, therefore, the producing cause, the formed being that is the product, and the purpose of this product belong to the same order: mature dogs generate puppies whose purpose is to develop into mature dogs. For living things, the goal is actualization according to a specific form, as this is the fundamental orientation at the heart of the being.

In living things, form is the very life of the being, the principle that organizes and dictates the development of matter.[55] The form of the rose is the life of the rose, since this life organizes the leaves, the stem, etc., in a way specific to roses, and dictates the way in which the rose develops. As long as the rose is alive, the rose behaves according to its form. However, when the rose dies, it loses its form, its life, and so the being disintegrates and is no longer properly a rose. It may be called a "dead rose," but this is misleading. A rose is (like any being) form and matter, but form in the case of a rose (and other living beings) is much more than shape. Form is life, the organizing principle that is the inherent principle of motion of the being. Accordingly, a "dead rose" is not really a rose but rather a body that retains, for the time being and not much longer, the shape once attained by a real rose, a living rose, which only as living could have attained the shape that is now observed. In being the principle of development, form is also the cause of the shape, in the case of living things. On the other hand, in artificial things, form is simply the shape imposed on the matter by the

55. See *De Anima* 2.1.

maker for a certain purpose. In the case of a saddle, form is simply the arrangement of the leather.

Forms organize matter. Forms are also the fruition or actualization of matter, since a form emerges from a material subject as this subject moves from a potential to an actual state. In change with qualification, as when a dog changes not as such but only in terms of size or color, etc., the new form(s) acquired by the subject change the being of the subject only in a certain respect. In change without qualification, which is coming into being or passing away, the very acquisition or loss of form entails the subject's acquisition or loss of being. In this latter type of change, the form that is acquired or lost is substantial to the being. As noted, in the case of living things, this form is the life specific to the being. Hence, when a dog is generated, the generated dog has received dog-life—its form—from its parents, and this form governs its being as it grows, develops, and behaves in a way specific to dogs. The dog is an individual, however, because his form emerges from a particular material subject. This subject is the biological material that was in potency to becoming the given dog and that actually became this dog when dog-life was generated from it. Through generation, the now living subject possesses the principle of motion and development that is specific to dogs within itself. This latter sense of form—namely, species—is the fundamental principle of natural things. Nature is fundamentally form. Each (natural) thing has its own specific form—its own nature—that governs its motion and being.

I.3d
The Human Form and Knowledge

Aristotle applies his same principles of matter and form, first developed in his account of change, to the human being. The human soul is the form of the body, and the goal of the human being is actualization according to its form. The human form, like other forms, emerges from the potency of matter, and so the human form (the soul) is truly at its natural place with the human body. In this respect, Aristotle differs from Plato, who emphasizes the affinity of the soul with a transcendent realm. Aristotle does emphasize that the human soul's proper activities are thinking and knowing. For human life is distinguished specifically by these activities, not by nutrition and growth (which it shares with plants and animals), and not by sense perception (which it shares with the other animals).[56] Human beings are defined as rational animals, since the use of reason distinguishes human life from other animals.

That which is specific to a thing defines the thing as a whole. For example, the square shares three sides with the triangle, but the possession of the fourth side determines the entire configuration of the square, and all its sides, in a new way, in a way proper and specific to the square.[57] So, too, the possession of reason in human beings not only adds a new dimension on top of the levels shared with other living things. The possession of reason determines human life as a whole, since it determines the human being as a specific kind of nutritive, growing, and perceiving animal, namely, as a rational animal. The human soul is properly the rational soul, since the body, as well as all dimensions of human life, are ordered for the sake of reason. However, Aristotle interprets the significance of reason and thinking in his own way.

First, to Aristotle, the intelligible realm is to a significant degree contained in the sensible realm, since forms exist in matter. In considering forms, the mind does not need to connect with a realm that is above the human mind. On the contrary, the mind is the very realm in which the forms exist as universal realities. Outside the mind, however, forms exist only in individuals, just as the form of dog exists only in individual dogs. True, the species of dog does exist, but not separately from individual dogs. Rather, this species exists because individual dogs, in generating other individual dogs, transmit their specific form. However, the mind can understand the concept "dog" universally, without necessarily imagining or sensing an individual dog, as when we understand the judgment "All dogs are animals." Unlike sensing and imagining, which always grasp what is individual (I see or imagine this particular red color, hear or imagine this particular sound, etc.), understanding grasps universals (I understand the universal meaning of "red," the universal meaning of "sound," etc.).

But how does the form, which exists only in individuals, become universal in the mind? When we sense, the chief cause of the sensation is the object sensed, which sends some information to our sense faculty. For example, when someone makes a noise, the noise causes us to hear it, whether we want to or not (if there is no obstruction). The noise heard comes from

---

56. *Nicomachean Ethics* 1.7.1097b33–1098a8.

57. Aristotle makes this analogy between levels of soul and figures in *De Anima* 2.3.414b20–32.

whatever made the sound. Naturally, our hearing needs to function in order to receive the noise, but our capacity to hear is not sufficient in order to hear the noise. Hence sensation comes from the sensible objects, not from our very senses. In the case of thinking, the case is different. For although the action of the sensible object (and a functioning sense) is sufficient to cause sensation in us, the presence of an object is not sufficient to cause thinking. The reason is that every sensible object is individual. Of itself, the object can only transmit to us its own reality, which is that of individualized form, not that of universal form. Producing the universal form in the mind must be the work of the intellect. The intellect is able to draw out from individuals the universal form, is able to extract the common form from the individual conditions in which the form exists in the sensible world. Hence thinking differs from sensing because thinking is the product of the intellect, while sensing is not the product of the sense organ. That is why we can think at will, but not sense at will. Having experienced sensible objects is necessary for subsequent understanding of their universal forms, but the act of thinking is produced by the thinking mind itself. Conversely, a functioning sense organ is necessary for sensation, but sensation is produced by the action of the sensible object upon the organ.

In an important sense, the intellect is a potential principle. For the intellect assimilates or receives these forms when the intellect understands them, when the intellect moves from the state of not understanding to the state of actual understanding. In other words, the intellect is informed, in a way analogous to how matter is informed. Actual understanding implies that the intellect assimilates the universal form that is understood. However, although the intellect is a potential principle, the intellect cannot be material. For any material thing is determinate, and therefore has determinate potentiality. For example, clay is a determinate substance that is in potency to a variety of shapes; however, clay does not have the potency to produce laughter or justice, precisely because of its determinate nature and potency. The intellect, however, is in potency to anything that is intelligible. The intellect's potency is indeterminate, and prior to understanding the intellect is not a determinate nature, but rather only a potential principle that is able to assume any intelligible form. In other words, the intellect must be immaterial. Although it is potential, the intellect is not material, precisely because its potentiality is pure.[58]

58. See ibid., 3.4.

However, the intellect has the power to universalize the forms, to purify them from their material and individual conditions, so that they can be understood. In this sense, the intellect is an active principle, a principle that generates. The intellect's capacity for abstraction bespeaks its divine character, because of all things in nature the intellect is the only thing that can, in a sense, actualize itself. Since nothing can actualize itself unless it is already actual in some respect (otherwise something would come from nothing), this means that the intellect possesses an element that is always actual, that is eternal and, in this sense, divine. This is the only immortal aspect of the soul, according to Aristotle, as he intimates in a brief passage (*De Anima*, book III, chapter 5). However, the full meaning of Aristotle's remarks on human immortality remained a question for his students and commentators. Moreover, his doctrine of the intellect in its two aspects— namely, the possible (or potential) intellect and the active intellect (as they have come to be known)—continues to be a source of debate and reflection.

I.3e
The Goal of the Human Form

What is clear is Aristotle's emphasis on intellectual activity as the proper human activity, and as the activity that assimilates human beings to the eternal and divine. Human beings, like all beings, seek actualization according to their form. The form proper to human beings is the rational soul, so the actualization that is most proper to human beings is intellectual actualization, namely, growth in knowledge. The best kind of intellectual actualization is found in the best kind of knowledge, namely wisdom, the knowledge of first principles and causes.

Love of wisdom is a desire for the divine and eternal, according to Aristotle. This is a desire to strengthen the divine element in humanity, and a desire to contemplate divine things.[59] Since understanding entails assimilation between knower and known, this desire to understand the divine is a desire to assimilate it. However, this is not a desire to lose oneself through complete union with God. Nor is it a desire to return to a source, as in Plato. In the first place, human beings, like all other beings, seek actualization according to their specific form, namely, at their own level. They seek the best condition that is proper to them. Indeed, human beings seek knowledge of first causes and principles. However, this is a desire for the best form of

59. See *Nicomachean Ethics* 10.7.1177b26–1178a9.

human intellectual excellence. After all, the human intellect does have a divine spark, since it is, in a sense, subsistent actuality. However, this desire cannot reach beyond the bounds of one's specific form, since this would be the desire to become a different nature—a strange desire indeed, according to Aristotelian principles.[60] For, as explained, the inclination for actualization at the heart of beings stems from the very nature of their potencies. Nature, after all, is the very principle of movement inherent in a subject. Hence this inclination cannot exceed the bounds of the nature, since the nature dictates the inclination in the first place.

Secondly, according to Aristotle, there is no absolute creative source of reality to which the soul seeks to return. His analysis of change implies that the universe is eternal. For every change presupposes a subject that can change (as explained above). The subject, as changeable, came into being, and coming into being is a change that presupposes another subject. This latter subject can change and in turn also came into being, which implies another subject, and so on infinitely. What applies to coming into being also applies to passing away, since passing away is a change, which always presupposes a subject.[61] Since change is eternal, the universe that contains change is also eternal.

By definition, no perishable cause can sustain this eternal process of coming to be and passing away. Rather, something eternal must sustain eternal change.[62] Every motion depends on an actual mover. If this mover is itself moved, another actual mover is necessary. Ultimately, a first mover that is by nature unmoved is necessary to sustain all motion. Otherwise, there would be an infinite regress of moved movers.[63] In this impossible case, motion would not exist, since there would be no first actual mover to cause motion. The evidence of motion implies an eternal cause of motion. This eternal cause must be unmoved, incapable of change of any kind. In other words, this mover lacks potency, and its essence is actuality. But how does something unmoved move other things? The final cause or purpose of a thing moves the thing, while the cause remains unmoved. For example, an object of desire draws the agent, although the object itself does not move

60. Even when discussing humanity's assimilation to the divine through the element of reason, Aristotle stresses his general principle that what is proper to each thing is by nature best and most pleasant. See ibid., 10.7.1178a3–6.

61. See his analysis in *Physics* 8.1.

62. See ibid., 6.258b10–259a15.

63. See, e.g., ibid., 5.256a21–b4.

in this respect. All things seek and move toward actuality (according to their specific forms). The unmoved mover, which is essentially actuality, is that for the sake of which all things ultimately move. This eternal actuality is necessary to sustain the eternal process of particular actualizations of particular potencies. Moreover, this cause, as devoid of matter and potency, is a subsistent intellect, which, in sustaining actualization, sustains the order and intelligibility of a world governed by immanent forms.

As noted, for Aristotle our earthly world of generation and corruption, the sublunary world, depends on a cause that sustains this eternal process of change.[64] Similarly, in his geocentric astronomy, every sphere of the heavens depends on a cause that sustains its eternal (rotational) motion, since even the perfect motion of the heavenly bodies, which is uniform and circular, is an actualization of potency.[65] Since every sphere has its proper motion, every sphere depends on its unmoved mover. Ultimately, however, the whole hierarchical order of motions in the universe depends on a first cause, a first unmoved mover. This first unmoved mover, the highest and purest actuality, is also the ultimate end, the last final cause—that for the sake of which all things ultimately move.[66]

All things move according to their respective forms, their organizing principles. Things seek, not actuality as such, but the actuality of their specific forms, even though the whole universe, the whole order of forms, depends on a first unmoved mover—the highest actuality. God, this highest actuality, also has a proper activity. God does govern all things, since he ultimately orders all motion. However, he is not a creative source that brings things into existence out of itself. He only influences lower things through intermediary causes. All things point toward the first unmoved mover, since he is the ultimate final cause. However, the unmoved mover only concerns himself with the highest and best, namely, himself. God, the highest intellect, is thought thinking itself, rather than lower things. For the proper activity of the first cause must be proportionate to its nature. Hence the first cause, who is subsistent thought, must think only of the eternal

64. Some students of Aristotle, such as Avicenna and Averroes, interpreted the agent intellect mentioned in *De Anima* as the proximate cause of sublunary generation and corruption, even though they did not equate the agent intellect with the first cause (the first unmoved mover). This interpretation was not uncommon among medieval Jewish and Islamic philosophers.

65. See his discussion of rotational motion in *Physics* 8.8–9.

66. See *Metaphysics* 12.7.

and divine, since thinking about mutable and varying things would alter its nature.[67]

I.3f
Excellence and Desire for Actualization

Love of wisdom in Aristotle is the human desire for expansion or actualization according to the rational soul, the human form, rather than the desire to return to an absolute source. This is equivalent to the desire for virtue or excellence, since excellence is for a being its best and most developed mode of actualization, its best condition or state. Hence this desire is also the desire for happiness, the final end—what people pursue for its own sake, while everything else is done for the sake of happiness. Human excellence has two fundamental dimensions, namely, unity and knowledge.

In the *Nicomachean Ethics*, Aristotle points out that the goal of anything with a function is to perform its function well. For example, the function of a lyre player is to play the lyre, while his goal is to play it well. The function of a living thing is not simply to live, since life is what plants and animals have in common. Rather, the function of each living thing is to live the life determined by its specific form. In the case of human beings, their function is to live the life determined by the rational soul. Accordingly, their purpose—their fulfillment, their good, their happiness—is to live this life well. Although human beings share nutrition, growth, and perception with other living things, it is reason that both distinguishes and determines the human form.[68]

Hence, living the life proper to human beings well or excellently consists in the proper development of the rational soul. Since the rational soul includes two chief parts, both parts need to be developed in the proper way in order to achieve human excellence or virtue. The first part is reason, in the proper sense of the word. With reason, in this sense, human beings understand concepts and make judgments and inferences. The excellence of this part is knowledge, while its vice is ignorance. Accordingly, the different intellectual virtues correspond to the different areas of human knowledge, such as art, science, and wisdom. The second part, although not reason in the proper sense of the word, relates to reason. This part includes emotions and appetites—the various motives for action—that may either agree or

67. See ibid., 12.9.1074b25–34.

68. *Nicomachean Ethics* 1.7.

conflict with reason. This is practical reason, which always combines reason and desire, the means and the goal of an action.[69]

This latter part determines a person's character, since a person's character disposes the person to behave and act in a certain way and to pursue some things but avoid other things. Accordingly, a good character possesses good desires that are in line with correct reasoning; both desire and reasoning need to operate well. The excellence of this part of the rational soul is obedience to correct reason, while vice in this case is disobedience to reason. Accordingly, the different moral virtues correspond to the different ways in which the emotions and appetites obey sound reason. For example, courage is the proper regulation of the feelings of fear and confidence, while temperance is the proper regulation of the appetites. In moral virtue, emotions and appetites are in a state of well-being, since they are well regulated in obeying sound reason. There is a proud sense of accomplishment in having the strength to do what one knows is correct (courage), and there is physical well-being in proportioned eating and drinking, and generally in the proper rule of bodily appetites (temperance). In virtue, pleasure and knowledge coincide, since emotions and appetites have learned to agree with reason—the whole character is working at its best. On the other hand, emotions and appetites that have been nurtured in the wrong way—that have become too extreme—demand gratification at the expense of reason. For example, the coward gratifies and justifies his irrational fears, and in so doing fails to do what is best for himself and others, since he fails to promote the best state of his soul, and others cannot depend on him. On the other hand, the rash person also fails (himself and others), but for different reasons, namely, for gratifying the thrill of uncalculated risk.

All the moral virtues presuppose the virtue of prudence (*phronesis*), which is sound reasoning to reach good ends.[70] Prudence is both an intellectual and a moral virtue, since it is the necessary intellectual aspect of moral virtue. At the same time, prudence (in the proper sense of the word) also includes the moral virtues, since intelligence without moral desires is mere cleverness. The right goal (determined by good desire), as well as the knowledge of the means to the goal (practical reasoning), are necessary for acting and living well. If any of these elements is lacking, it is impossible to cultivate the moral virtues.[71] Prudence is equivalent to practical

69. See ibid., 13.1103a1–10.

70. See ibid., 6.13.1144b30–1145a6.

71. Both art and prudence are types of "know-how," since they both pursue means

wisdom, namely, the knowledge of how to live well. For the person who attains virtue assigns to himself or herself the greatest of goods.

The moral virtues are the proper actualization of the character, while the intellectual virtues are the proper actualization of the intellect. The attainment of both types of virtue entails unity in the soul. The intellect is shaped through teaching and study, while the character is shaped by actions. In the rest of this section, we will discuss the virtues of character; we shall deal with intellectual virtue in the next section.

A person becomes courageous by performing courageous actions and temperate by performing temperate actions.[72] Actions always leave a residue in the character, so that the more a person acts in a certain way, the more disposed the person becomes to act that way. This is similar to physical exercise, whereby the more a person exercises, the more the person can exercise. In other words, performing activities develops our capacities or dispositions—our potentiality. In the moral life, performing virtuous actions generates virtue of character, which is the disposition or habit to behave virtuously. The virtues are habits. Hence acting virtuously is not necessarily equivalent to the possession of virtue, since vicious people do a good action sometimes. Only the person who acts virtuously out of habit is truly virtuous. As possessor of the habit, such a person enjoys acting virtuously (and therefore pursues virtue for its own sake) and knows how to act virtuously in specific circumstances. For example, the temperate person enjoys eating healthy foods in the right way and can make healthy choices—desires are in line with good reasoning.

Even though acting well is the first necessary step towards virtue, the full attainment of virtue consists in the pleasure of virtue.[73] Unlike natural faculties, such as sight, whereby the potentiality precedes activity in the order of development,[74] actions generate dispositions or habits. In this latter case, activity precedes potentiality or capacity. In a word, moral virtue is the proper actualization of the character, whereby the appetites and emotions

---

for the sake of ends. However, in the case of prudence, the chief element is intending the right end, while in the case of art, the chief element is knowledge of the means. Hence, Aristotle points out that in the moral life an unwilling mistake is preferable to an intended evil, while the artist who errs intentionally in his art is a better artist than an artist who makes a mistake through ineptitude. See ibid., 6.5.1140b23–24.

72. See ibid., 2.1.

73. See ibid., 2.3.

74. The embryo only has the potentiality to see, but is not able to do so. After developing, sight and seeing ensue.

are in line with correct reasoning, whereby the soul agrees with itself. This state is most pleasant, since the whole soul is satisfied and at peace. The pleasure of excellence is also the best and most genuine pleasure, since it is the enjoyment of living and acting well, of functioning well as a rational animal. In this case, pleasure consolidates, preserves, and promotes excellence, since the virtuous person, in finding pleasure in the virtuous life, chooses virtue for its own sake.

However, pleasure is a double-edged sword, since pleasure can also promote and preserve vice. The pleasure of vice is the pleasure of ineptitude. This is a fragmented pleasure that, ultimately, divides and torments the soul.[75] The chief problem with vice is that, like any fully acquired habit, it is pleasant to the possessor. Vicious people have learned, through repeated actions, to enjoy behaving badly, so that their pleasure gratifies them while it enslaves them to an unsound constitution. In finding pleasure in vice, vicious people choose it regularly and for its own sake, and their vice increases accordingly.

This is similar to ineptitude in a craft or sport. A tennis player who has developed a deeply engrained bad technique is most comfortable playing according to his bad habits, which perpetuates his ineptitude. Gratifying the pleasures of his bad tennis habits comes at the expense of playing badly and unsuccessfully. His being as a tennis player is divided, since one part of him (his habits) lead him to play in a certain way, while another part of him (his desire for excellence) despises his own impulses and reactions. In order to become a better player, he must first understand the proper technique (through some type of instruction), and begin to play according to the new technique. Since he is not used to playing in this way, initially this will require extreme concentration and patience in order to avoid the recurrence of his old tendencies, which even in the best cases do recur occasionally and cause setbacks. Only after a sustained period of repeated tennis playing according to the new technique will the player begin to grow comfortable in this new pattern. And only after the new technique has left a deep enough imprint in his disposition as a tennis player, so that the player enjoys his new style, will the player possess good tennis habits and begin to cultivate true excellence in his sport. Only then will he reach the good—performing his function well. Only then will he enjoy his sport fully, in the best way.

75. For Aristotle, as for Plato, virtue is the soul's inner friendship, while vice is discord or war within the soul. Virtue is also the basis for true friendship with others. See *Nicomachean Ethics* 9.4.

Similarly, even though morally vicious people enjoy their vice, and thus have a mistaken view of the good life, their pleasure can never be as complete as the pleasure of functioning as excellent human beings. Hence actualization in vice is never as rewarding as actualization in excellence, so that even vicious constitutions ultimately seek virtue (unconsciously in some cases), since their lives are unfulfilling attempts to reach true fulfillment. Since virtue is the best form of human actualization, human nature tends toward virtue more than vice, even though human nature has the capacity for both. Similarly, the body tends toward health more than disease, in the sense that health is its good and its strength, even though the body can be corrupted by disease and unhealthy living. Human nature ultimately tends toward virtue, since virtue is the goal of the human function, namely, to function properly as a rational animal. This is true, ironically, even though in some times and places the vicious outnumber the virtuous, since the basic orientation of human nature—actualization according to its form—remains. Similarly, one might say that even though mediocre tennis players outnumber the excellent ones, the goal of a tennis player as such is to play excellently.

Changing the habits that determine one's character may be possible, but it is not easy, since this requires taking a new and (at least initially) painful path on a consistent basis. Some habits are so engrained that even the best efforts result in new behavior, perhaps, but not in its enjoyment (which makes the new pattern weak, easily suppressed by the old one). In some extreme cases, however, the person can no longer change.[76] That is why early education in virtue is fundamental, since the habits formed at an early age take the greatest hold on the character.[77]

Accordingly, acquiring the moral virtues requires actualizing the character in the proper way through concrete activities. Moreover, the virtues require continual cultivation throughout life, since, although acting badly occasionally is still possible for a good person, repeatedly acting badly corrupts virtue. Prudence or practical wisdom (which includes all the moral virtues) requires a lifelong commitment.[78]

---

76. Still, for Aristotle people are ultimately responsible for these states of character, since their actions led to them. See ibid., 3.5.1114a3–23.

77. Ibid., 2.1.1103b24–26.

78. What was said above in regard to Plato (section I.2d) also may be said here in regard to Aristotle: "Nevertheless virtue is more stable than vice, since unity is more stable than disunity. The more virtuous a soul is, the stronger is its tendency to remain in the one state in which it is meant to be."

Therefore, a fundamental aspect of Aristotle's love of wisdom is his emphasis on the human drive to live well, since this is the proper actualization of the human form, whereby the soul is unified, happy, strong, and ordered to reason. This drive is philosophical insofar as proper actualization requires the pursuit of knowledge about what is good for the person and the community, as well as the development of the proper habits that support this knowledge.

I.3g
Wisdom as the Highest Mode of Actualization

However, even though moral virtue is fundamental in living well, the highest expression of love of wisdom in Aristotle consists in the intellectual virtues, since these are most proper to reason itself, the highest part of the soul. As noted, the moral virtues include intellectual virtue, specifically prudence, which is wisdom ordered to action. Similarly, art is an intellectual virtue that is ordered to performance or production. In prudence and art, reason is still working for an end other than pure knowledge (reason's proper end and highest fulfillment). Hence, these virtues are not the highest expression and actualization of the rational soul. Rather, this highest expression and actualization consists in the pursuit of knowledge for its own sake, in knowledge of the greatest truths. Accordingly, although practical wisdom is fundamental, theoretical contemplation (the pursuit of wisdom in the proper sense) is happiness in the strict sense of the word.[79]

For this knowledge, in considering first principles and causes, expands the intellect to the highest degree and assimilates human nature to the divine nature more than any other activity. Moreover, theoretical contemplation, seeking truth for its own sake, is an activity that finds its end in itself. It is the most immanent of all human activities, whereby the result of the activity is purely the strengthening of the activity—growth in knowledge—unlike practical activities, which yield external results. Moreover, due to its immanence and independence of external things, theoretical contemplation is the activity most in our control, as well as the activity that can be pursued most extensively throughout life.[80]

---

79. See his discussion in *Nicomachean Ethics* 10.6–8.

80. Thinking and the pursuit of truth are, of all activities, least dependent on the body, so we can engage in them in youth and old age.

Due to its self-sufficient purity, whereby it is purely its own end—knowledge for the sake of knowledge—theoretical contemplation can accommodate the greatest pleasure. For pleasure only exists in activities, and so is distinguished according to activities—the pleasure of conversation is different from the pleasure of music, etc. Hence the quality of the pleasure depends on the quality of the activity in which it is found. Fragmented and dependent activities yield only fragmented and dependent pleasures. Theoretical contemplation, however, yields to rational animals the purest, most immanent, most self-sufficient, and most proper pleasure. Accordingly, theoretical contemplation is the greatest and most pleasant form of human fulfillment, since it is the actualization of the highest dimension of reason.

Moreover, Aristotle identifies the fruition of theoretical contemplation with the pleasure of possessing the truth. For even though mortals may be called wise only with qualifications, human beings can obtain at least some truths of wisdom, specifically understanding their experience through causes, even though they are not able to understand divine things in themselves. Hence this highest pleasure, the pleasure of possessing (some) truths of wisdom, is a serene pleasure, a restful beholding of the truth, whereby the theoretical activity truly finds its rest within itself.[81] Aristotelian love of wisdom attains its highest fulfillment in this serene beholding, which is also the purest expansion of reason, the human form.

In this exalted sense, Aristotle's love of wisdom transforms itself from a seeking into a possessing, and in this regard one sees a fundamental difference between the Aristotelian love of wisdom, on the one hand, and the Platonic and Socratic loves of wisdom, on the other. In the latter cases, love of wisdom is always a seeking, due to their own conceptions of the soul and knowledge. In the broad sense, however, Aristotle remains fundamentally a lover of wisdom, since he emphasizes the necessity to cultivate both moral and intellectual virtue throughout life. Virtue remains, even for the truly noble, a task to be lived, day after day. The peculiar features of Aristotle's love of wisdom stem from the roots of this love and from his philosophical method. Aristotle's desire to understand the world of change and sense, on its own terms and in the most comprehensive way, led him to his own conception of the human soul and to a new conception of human wisdom. Human wisdom is now the highest expression of an immanent form, the rational soul. Since the human soul, like other forms, develops from a

---

81. In this vein, he comments that those who know will experience greater pleasure than those who inquire. See *Nicomachean Ethics* 10.7.1177a27–28.

potential principle, its orientation is not otherworldly, but rather according to its specific nature and at its own level. In human wisdom, there is the recognition of the limits of human knowledge as such, but there is also the recognition that human excellence (including theoretical knowledge) is an adequate and rightly earned possession for the human essence. For human excellence is specific to rational animals, not an inadequate approximation of a transcendent standard. Accordingly, human beings who have attained the best condition according to the human form deserve to be called wise, with the qualification that their wisdom is a wisdom rooted in the human essence. It is not divine wisdom.

At the same time, human wisdom is the true fulfillment of the human essence, whose goal is actualization according to its specific form, not according to some transcendent standard. In Aristotle, therefore, one finds a love of wisdom that is in every respect its own end, since this is the pursuit of excellence that yields, through continual exertion, the very actualization that is the immanent goal of the human form. In Aristotle, love of wisdom is truly the desire to become more of what one already is. In this regard, and with all the aforementioned qualifications, Aristotelian love of wisdom can aspire to possess its goal in the human sphere, since its impulse is not reaching out to the transcendent but rather drawing out from its own essence in order to expand according to this essence. Interestingly, this immanent impulse does result in the discovery of the divine, in the recognition of the spiritual nature of the human soul and in the discovery and assimilation of higher intellectual substances.

I.4

THE CORE OF ANCIENT GREEK LOVE OF WISDOM

Even though Socrates, Plato, and Aristotle identify the human drive for wisdom with principles consistent with their respective philosophical outlooks, there are basic commonalities among the Socratic, Platonic, and Aristotelian versions of love of wisdom. First, ancient Greek love of wisdom is complete love. In other words, it is a love that, as rooted in and as expressive of the whole self, seeks the fulfillment of the whole self. For Socrates, Plato, and Aristotle identify love of wisdom with the basic human desire for happiness, which they understand as comprehensive well-being, as genuine fulfillment. To them, philosophy is the activity most conducive to happiness. Hence, a fundamental dimension of love of wisdom is the pursuit of excellence, both moral and intellectual. This requires the proper cultivation of the soul—the true self, not only in terms of reason and knowledge but also in terms of the character. This comprehensive cultivation of the soul leads to overall satisfaction and well-being. Moreover, virtue is to these thinkers the integration of the human self, the state whereby the soul governs itself properly and is, thereby, most autonomous and free. A chief aspect of love of wisdom is this core human drive for wholeness or unity, for inner plenitude, for genuine strength of soul, and for the fulfillment that comes only with this state of being. Only the genuinely complete self can enjoy complete fulfillment, complete pleasure, complete well-being. Accordingly, to love wisdom is to love virtue.

Since love of wisdom is not only the desire for knowledge but also the desire to live well, love of wisdom promotes being well (inner virtue) and acting well (social/political virtue). The individual and the social aspects of virtue are inseparable, since the rule of reason ensures the order of the soul, as well as the social order. The soul is ordered through living and acting well, and a well-ordered soul is most conditioned to live and act well—you become what you do, and you act according to what you have become. The individual good is, ultimately, inseparable from the social good; to cultivate one is to cultivate the other, to neglect one is to neglect the other. The person who has found true contentment, by having shaped his or her soul according to the rule of reason, is least likely to encroach upon others, to neglect the rights of others. Rather, this person is best equipped for true friendship and for promoting the good of the community as a whole. In short, the virtuous person is both happy and just.

Secondly, in addition to the desire for the freedom found in the autonomy of reason, which is the proper order of the rational soul, ancient Greek love of wisdom is a desire for the freedom and happiness of truth. In the first sense of freedom, when reason becomes free to rule the soul, the whole soul experiences the freedom of contentment, of living and acting the way the soul wants, not just with a part of itself but its whole being. In the second sense of freedom, reason pursues the truth for its own sake and seeks the liberation and fulfillment that only truth can provide it, since reason's highest aspiration is truth concerning the most important questions. This is certainly part of the good life as a whole. However, this is a dimension of reason that goes beyond reason's rule of the whole soul. Rather, this is reason's desire for its proper end—knowledge of the truth for its own sake.

Love of wisdom, in this sense, is reason's desire to reach the highest truths, which ultimately pertain to divine being.

Through the desire for the freedom of truth, love of wisdom constantly seeks to break its own limitations, its own bondage, as it reaches out for the eternal and divine. The nature of this drive for freedom is clearly expressed in Plato and in Aristotle. Plato describes it as the soul's desire to liberate itself from the sensible realm in order to reach the pure forms; to the extent that the soul has not reached its goal, it remains restless, precisely due to its bondage. Aristotle describes it as the soul's core desire to engage in the activity that is most for its own sake, that is most self-sufficient and free—the contemplation of the noblest realities. Through this activity above all others, the soul experiences true freedom, since thinking finds its end in the very act of thinking, as well as its best and most proper satisfaction. At the same time, this activity is the highest mode of actualization and, thereby, the freest expansion of the human form. This drive is also clearly discernible in Socrates' relentless pursuit of truth for its own sake: the value of learned ignorance is, at its core, emancipation from unexamined living. Moreover, he does mention duty to the divine as an important aspect of his pursuit of wisdom. Socratic philosophy is also inspired by the superiority of divine wisdom.

In this second sense, as the drive for truth itself, ancient Greek love of wisdom is also a complete love. That is, it is the desire for comprehensive understanding, understanding of the meaning and purpose of life. In terms of what we know about Socrates, the emphasis is more specifically on the human sphere, while Plato and Aristotle also include other subjects, such as cosmology and metaphysics, which situate the human sphere within the greater framework of reality. But all three seek ultimate meaning. Even though Plato investigates particular forms, he traces all the forms back to the Good, the source and goal of all things. Aristotle is indeed also a scientist and a specialist, but he ranks wisdom above science, since wisdom understands all things in light of first principles and causes. Moreover, even though he engages in specialized branches of research, he uses his four causes in all areas, and his goal is to understand each subject in light of the chief cause, namely, the final cause—the purpose or goal. In other words, Aristotle seeks meaning and purpose—marks of wisdom—even in specialized branches. For example, the central task in his treatment of matter in the *Physics* is not the exhaustive analysis of matter as such. Rather, his emphasis is on the purposive orientation of matter. In this sense, the various Aristotelian sciences support and find their fruition in Aristotelian wisdom, while wisdom captures the ultimate significance of all modes of knowledge.

Accordingly, the ultimate aim of ancient Greek love of wisdom in its Socratic, Platonic, and Aristotelian versions is fundamental, comprehensive knowledge. In this sense, it is a complete love that seeks complete knowledge. Moreover, as was seen, this classic love of wisdom is also complete love in another sense: the drive of the whole soul for self-integration, for completion and unity. This drive stems from the whole soul (reason and character) and aims at the well-being of the soul as a whole. In both senses, love of wisdom is a desire for freedom—for the freedom of truth in the one case, and for the freedom of the rule of reason in the other case. In both senses, love of wisdom is also a desire for happiness—for the happiness found in reason's fulfillment in (comprehensive) truth in the one case, and for the happiness found in the soul's contentment through virtue in the other case. In a word, ancient Greek love of wisdom is complete love for complete fulfillment.

The common core of ancient Greek love of wisdom remains in the Middle Ages (with revision and development), but it is in stark contrast with the philosophical desire characteristic of the modern period. New spiritual possibilities of ancient Greek love of wisdom are discovered and developed in the medieval period, when, informed by scriptural revelation, love of wisdom acquires a new meaning. Medieval love of wisdom interprets and grounds itself on new principles, giving new significance to this core human drive. Since medieval love of wisdom generally favors either Platonic or Aristotelian principles, we will examine both forms in the next chapter. In the third and last chapter, we will examine chief modern versions of philosophical desire. This presentation of different positions will continue to include reflection on basic alternatives regarding philosophical desire and pursuits. This reflection is also present in the Conclusion, along with a recapitulation.

Chapter 2

Medieval Love of Wisdom

The influence of Socrates, Plato, and Aristotle is incalculable. They spawned a variety of sects, schools, and systems in the Greek and Roman worlds; their legacy inspired the medieval tradition and beyond, continuing to this day. Even though Socrates left no writings, he was a model for conduct among Cynics, Stoics, Skeptics, and Epicureans, and his presence has remained alive, primarily through Plato's writings. Greek Neoplatonists, such as Plotinus (204/5–270) and Proclus (412–485), systematized teachings gathered from Plato's various dialogues into sophisticated metaphysical frameworks that also drew from Aristotle and that had profound influence in later theology and philosophy. In the Middle Ages, when scholars gained access to Aristotle's texts, the commentary on Aristotle quickly became the chief philosophical genre into the Renaissance.

In terms of the present work's focus on love of wisdom, it is not possible (nor is it necessary) to examine all the different philosophies inspired by Socrates, Plato, and Aristotle, just as it was not possible (or necessary) to examine all philosophers before Socrates. Socrates, Plato, and Aristotle were examined because each of them stands out as a distinct and exemplary version of love of wisdom. Because they profoundly drew from, developed, and illuminated a dimension of human desire that has perennial significance, they have perennial value. The same criteria will guide us in this chapter, as well as in the next. Which thinkers enrich our understanding and appreciation of love of wisdom, regardless (or even because) of alleged shortcomings?

In this regard, a great variety of thinkers from different traditions may be relevant, and the relevance may depend on one's background and affinities. In terms of what Socrates, Plato, and Aristotle stand for, they are neither unique nor the last word, even in their own tradition—they themselves followed models, helped many to channel their own philosophical vocations in new ways, and were also rejected by some. Even though many examples of love of wisdom could be included, the selection in this book depends (aside from the limited resources of the author) on two fundamental considerations. First, the philosophers included are major sources in the history of Western philosophy. Secondly, and more importantly, each of the philosophers included provides a distinct perspective on the question of love of wisdom, so that all of them together provide a helpful background for the reader wishing to approach this question for himself or herself.

In the medieval period, the two chief philosophical currents were the Platonic and the Aristotelian. These currents developed through translators, commentators, adapters, and synthesizers from the Greco-Roman and medieval worlds. These currents sometimes also assimilated elements from other schools, such as Stoicism. In spite of the various syntheses of Platonic and Aristotelian philosophy that were generated, the irreducible differences between these two outlooks remained. Accordingly, thinkers chose either Platonic or Aristotelian principles as their starting point, and when they synthesized they generally subordinated one approach to the other. For example, in one of the earlier and most influential syntheses, that of Plotinus, Aristotle's natural forms remain, but in a new light: Aristotle's forms participate in the Platonic forms. Although Aristotle is helpful in understanding the sensible world, Plato grasped the ultimate causes, according to Plotinus. Other thinkers saw the greater truths in Aristotelian terms, even as they used ideas associated with Plato. Accordingly, the following discussion of medieval love of wisdom will focus on these two dominating approaches during this period, the Platonic and the Aristotelian, as represented by two major thinkers. The work of St. Augustine (354–430), who lived during the last stage of classical antiquity, in many ways defines medieval Platonic love of wisdom (at least in the Christian tradition). Thomas Aquinas (1225–1274), the best-known philosopher and theologian from the medieval university tradition, well represents Aristotelian love of wisdom.[1]

1. In this university tradition, also known as Scholasticism, several important masters

However, before discussing the details of each thinker and the traditions they represent, another defining aspect of medieval love of wisdom must be mentioned.

According to Plato and Aristotle (and other great pagan thinkers from the Greco-Roman world), the lover of wisdom is, to speak redundantly, the philosopher (*philosopher* literally means lover of wisdom), namely, the person who cultivates reason in order to live excellently and pursue the truth about the most important questions. Plato and Aristotle discovered that an essential dimension of love of wisdom is the soul's desire to approach the divine and that wisdom, in the strict sense of the word, belongs to the divine rather than to mortals. Although they interpreted the soul's goal differently, and spoke of divine causes in different terms, both saw the universe as ultimately dependent upon one eternal and immaterial intelligence (which they identified with God), and both saw in human reason a spark of divine intelligence. This divine spark sets human beings apart from nonrational beings, but also indicates what is superior to the human realm. They interpret the ultimate goal of the soul as reaching towards the divine and see philosophy as the activity most conducive to this goal.

Medieval thinkers adopt some of these basic lines of thought, but with important changes. Reason, when properly used, can discover God to some extent, both as the cause of the universe and as the goal of the soul. Reason, properly used, can realize its own limits: wisdom, absolutely speaking, belongs to God rather than to human beings. Accordingly, to medieval thinkers of the Jewish, Christian, and Islamic traditions, reason, properly used, can and should welcome faith—faith in what God's wisdom has revealed to human beings through the prophets and the scriptures. To these medieval philosophers who are also people of a religion, God's superior wisdom is not only indicated to human beings through reason, which (like all things) ultimately comes from God. God's superior wisdom has also manifested itself through its special gift to humanity, namely, revelation.

---

such as St. Bonaventure still favored Augustine over the Aristotelian tradition, which they knew well. Thomas Aquinas' successor at the University of Paris, Henry of Ghent (ca. 1217–1293), well represents this mature phase of Augustinianism, since Henry addressed and incorporated Aristotle even more thoroughly than Bonaventure did. Like Aquinas, Henry synthesizes the Platonic and the Aristotelian traditions in light of the Christian faith. Unlike Aquinas, who favors Aristotle, Henry favors Plato as developed by Augustine. An account of Henry's synthesis in terms of love of wisdom is given in Flores, "The Roots of Love of Wisdom," 623–40.

Some of the revealed truths cannot be discovered through reason alone, but some of them may be discovered. For example, revelation mentions aspects of God's will and plans that cannot be determined through human reason alone. On the other hand, reason can discover some truths that also are mentioned in the scriptures, such as basic principles of right conduct. However, it is part of divine wisdom that all these things be included in the scriptures. For many people, who do not have the necessary leisure, preparation, or talent, are not able to arrive at various truths that could be reached through reason alone. Accordingly, divine wisdom revealed itself for the sake of guiding all humanity toward salvation, toward eternal life—the terms scripture uses to indicate the ultimate purpose of the soul. Divine wisdom manifests that human beings should prepare themselves for God, and that this is possible for everyone who lives as God commands, not only for those who cultivate reason according to philosophy.

Moreover, revelation also supports philosophy. After all, both revelation and reason come from God. Accordingly, revelation cannot conflict with reason. If there is an apparent conflict, this is due either to a misinterpretation of revelation (which should not be interpreted literally in every case), or to a misuse of reason, or both. Revelation, therefore, should confirm as well as orient reason. On the other hand, reason is essential to interpret scripture. Reason and revelation should mutually assist each other, for the sake of this life and the next, for the sake of truth itself. Within this general framework in which medieval thinkers operated, there is a good deal of variety, since for a given thinker the combination of reason and revelation depends on his own religious tradition as well as on his particular philosophical preferences.

In light of the aforementioned, we are in a better position to answer the following question: Who is the lover of wisdom, in this medieval context? The lover of wisdom is no longer, ironically, the pure philosopher, the person who relies only on the light of reason. The lover of wisdom is now the person who, in addition to the light of reason, also relies on revelation. For this person loves wisdom fully, including the added dimension of revealed divine wisdom (as found primarily in the scriptures), which was not accessible to the pagan philosophers. All the great medieval thinkers saw the coexistence of reason and revelation as superior to reason alone, and all of them studied the philosophical as well as their religious tradition. They all, to some extent, brought the insight of revelation to philosophical questions, and brought the resources of reason to the interpretation of revelation. Some of them were close to the pure philosophers of the classical tradition, while others saw themselves as theologians first.[2] All of them, however, valued and respected scripture and religious tradition, and they understood that these sources were not only irreplaceable by reason and philosophy but also necessary to facilitate for the majority that original and basic goal of philosophy—virtue. For the scriptures, unlike the arguments of the philosophers, communicate in many ways and at various levels, so that everyone can benefit from their teachings.

In terms of employing the resources of reason and revelation for the sake of greater insight into God, the world, and humanity, medieval love of wisdom will always be current. For anyone who seeks wisdom by synthesizing reason and religious tradition in some way is still to some extent working according to this medieval model. That this is no longer the chief model for the pursuit of wisdom is an interesting question in itself. As mentioned, a peculiar feature of medieval thought is the use of Greek philosophy, particularly Platonic and Aristotelian philosophy. As shall become evident in this chapter, especially in the last section, the ancient and medieval versions of love of wisdom share a basic core, in spite of their differences. Accordingly, the rejection of this core during the modern period is a rejection of both the ancient and the medieval models. We shall discuss the nature and implications of this rejection in chapter 3, as well as in the Conclusion. For now, the focus must be medieval love of wisdom itself, in its two chief forms.

II.1

MEDIEVAL PLATONIC LOVE OF WISDOM: AUGUSTINE

Even though very little from Plato's own writings was directly accessible in the medieval period, Plato's ideas were known and had profound influence. In the case of St. Augustine, who accessed Plato through Neoplatonists like Plotinus and Porphyry (ca. 234–ca. 305) and authorities like Cicero (106–43 BC), the encounter with Platonism was a defining moment, both

2. The Muslim philosopher Ibn Rushd (or Averroes), for example, considered philosophical knowledge as superior to theology. The same is true of the Jewish philosopher Gersonides and of several other Jewish and Islamic philosophers from the Middle Ages. On the other hand, St. Bonaventure, like many medieval Christian thinkers, placed theology above pure philosophy. A basic introduction to medieval philosophy and theology, which takes into account the Jewish, Christian, and Islamic traditions, is Brown and Flores, *Historical Dictionary of Medieval Philosophy and Theology.*

personally and historically. Augustine's synthesis of revelation and Platonic philosophy dominated Christian thought until the thirteenth century, when Latin translations of Aristotle provided another framework for Christian theologians. St. Thomas Aquinas, who will be discussed in the next main section, formulated the most influential version of Christian theology within this new, Aristotelian framework. Yet even when Aristotle had gained a strong foothold in European universities, Augustine still thrived, as may be seen in the writings of St. Bonaventure (d. 1274), Aquinas' contemporary at the University of Paris, and in those of Henry of Ghent (d. 1293), their immediate successor at Paris.[3] In the Middle Ages, Augustine's profound influence went beyond university walls, among Rhineland mystics and in the monastic tradition.

Even Thomas Aquinas, who favored Aristotle, still followed Augustine in important ways. And even though later Platonists like Bonaventure and Henry of Ghent were quite original, their philosophies still drew from the same vital source as Augustine, and in this regard (aside from doctrinal similarities) we are right in calling them Augustinian. For now, therefore, the purpose is to articulate the nature of that philosophical desire, of that love of wisdom, which originally possessed Augustine and which spawned the rich tradition called Augustinianism.

The work of Augustine draws from two fundamental sources. One of these sources is the central philosophical impulse exemplified by Plato (and Aristotle), namely, the desire for virtue and knowledge. The second source is faith, which takes ascendancy in Augustine precisely because of the insufficiency of the first source. Born of a pagan father and a Christian mother, Augustine's very self is the confluence of two different traditions, which, after much struggle, he managed to reconcile in his seminal synthesis of philosophy and faith. Augustine's experience with philosophy will be discussed first (in sections 1a and 1b), since this experience paved the way for his embracing of faith.

Augustine recognized within himself the powerful meaning of love of wisdom as a pursuit that never fully possesses its object. Although Augustine's own love of wisdom does share common vital sources with Plato's love of wisdom, Augustine's love of wisdom is also an original expression that is in one sense liberating, and in another sense tragic. Augustine recognizes in himself the two drives that fuel ancient Greek love of wisdom (summarized

---

3. A study of Henry of Ghent's thought is Flores, *Henry of Ghent: Metaphysics and the Trinity.*

at the end of chapter 1). First, the soul desires virtue—integration, completion, wholeness—and the peace and strength that come with it. He also recognizes that reason thirsts for truth as its ultimate satisfaction. The first drive seeks the freedom of well-being. The second seeks the liberation of truth. Augustine's life story, as found in his *Confessions*, is one of constant struggle in search for both virtue and truth, a personal quest for wisdom.

As explained in chapter 1, for Aristotle and Plato love of wisdom is the constant pursuit of virtue and knowledge. For them, although human beings remain, ultimately, lovers rather than possessors of wisdom, a life seeking wisdom is its own reward, since virtuous living and philosophical thinking are worthy in themselves. Moreover, Plato and Aristotle do speak, in their own terms, of the immortality of the soul, and of the fact that philosophy assimilates the soul to the divine, since philosophy considers eternal truths. Plato even speaks explicitly of philosophy as the life most deserving of rewards in the afterlife, and Aristotle claims that of all people the philosopher is happiest since he is most akin, and therefore dearest, to the gods.[4]

For his part, Augustine finds that love of wisdom in its two dimensions is tragic, if considered only from the standpoint of what human beings can achieve through their own efforts. For human beings, on their own, cannot achieve genuine virtue or knowledge. Augustine recognizes that a life in pursuit of virtue and knowledge is better than a life that neglects these ideals, but he does not find that the very pursuit of virtue and knowledge—the philosophical life—is sufficiently rewarding. On the contrary, the philosophical life shows the very weakness of human nature, its very incapacity to accomplish what it inherently desires.

II.1a
The Insufficiency of Practical Philosophy

First, no matter how accustomed the character may be, there is always in the soul the capacity to undermine virtue. Augustine recognizes in his own personal life, as well as in those around him, a powerful and self-asserting force that refuses to subject itself completely to reason: free will. Plato does not identify this force in these same terms. Plato speaks of the spirit as the motive force of the soul, and as the seat of the emotions. However, for Plato,

---

4. Plato expresses this, among other places, at the very end of *Republic*, while Aristotle makes this point in *Nicomachean Ethics* 10.8.1179a30–34.

the spirit is the natural ally of reason, and even though in many persons the spirit serves other ends aside from reason, the spirit is *meant* to serve reason.

In Greek philosophy, free choice is usually described in terms of practical reason: the intellect as ordered to actions. In this sense, free choice is characterized as a function of the intellect, rather than as an autonomous faculty. For Augustine, on the other hand, free choice is a function of the will, an autonomous faculty on a par with the intellect. Will and intellect are two faculties of the mind, and neither is reducible to the other. As Augustine puts it, you can know something and not love it, but you cannot love something that you do not know at all.[5] We also will to understand and understand that we will.[6] This shows both the distinction and coexistence of intellect and will, faculties of thinking and knowing, on the one hand, and loving and choosing, on the other.[7]

Free will can choose even what the person tries to reject, even what reason knows should be avoided,[8] despite extensive habituation. In these cases, the will is divided: it opposes itself by willing what it also does not will in some other respect. For Augustine, purely by human efforts the will cannot be healed completely, since it can resist reason even in the most virtuous souls. In this sense, the soul falls short of its goal, not merely because habituation in virtue is a lifelong commitment rather than a fixed state, but because of an inherent faculty—on account of human nature itself.

This does not mean that the will is inherently evil.[9] On the contrary, as the faculty of love and freedom, the will is essential for the purpose of the

5. See *The Trinity* 15.27.50.

6. *Confessions* 13.11.

7. Augustine's analysis is rather original, but this does not mean that these dimensions of human existence are completely absent from Greek philosophy, as is evident from chapter 1. Moreover, the treatments of intellect and will, in Augustine and in the medieval tradition, still rely to some extent on Greek philosophy. See Flores, "Love of Wisdom," 633. After Augustine, medieval philosophers of the Christian tradition tend to see the will as an autonomous faculty of the mind. However, they differ in terms of the ways in which they understand the coexistence of intellect and will in the mind, especially in terms of the importance they assign to each of these faculties. For many medieval followers of Augustine, the will is (in some respects) a higher faculty than the intellect. Others, who favor Aristotelian philosophy, tend to stress the superiority of the intellect.

8. See *Confessions* 8.5; 8.8–9.

9. Without free will, human beings could not live rightly. See *On Free Choice of the Will* 2.18–20.

soul, which is not only knowledge but also love of God and neighbor (charity). The will is made well when it clings to the highest Good—God, which is also the highest Truth. Then, the will rejoices in and follows the truth, and so agrees with reason. However, for the soul to reach this state of unity and enlightenment, it needs God's grace,[10] as explained more fully below.

In addition, Augustine understands the roles of appetites and emotions in the soul, as well as reason's capacity to guide the soul, in a more pessimistic way than Plato does. Appetites and emotions are forces that, even in the best psychic constitutions, can counteract reason. The human soul always retains inner tensions, and although the ideal of the soul is harmonious unity (i.e., virtue), this ideal condition is not attainable purely through the efforts of human nature. His conclusion is that human beings naturally desire what, tragically, is not available to them purely through nature.[11] The virtues are never fully experienced, let alone possessed.

For example, human temperance never takes the completed form of peaceful harmony. At best, temperance is the subjugation of the lower desires by the higher desires, since to Augustine the flesh and the spirit are at war.[12] Social justice is mixed with so many evils that its practice remains not only imperfect but also corrupt. First, reason can never assume total authority in matters of justice, since reason can only judge external actions. Moreover, judges pass judgment based on limited evidence (and sometimes even resort to unjust torture in an attempt to supplement their ignorance), never based on all the relevant circumstances, precedents, and facts. A so-called just war, for example, presupposes as much evil as it does justice. For in a just war, justice fights evil, while the war itself, with its terrible consequences, also causes evil. Courage, in particular, shows the evil mixed with virtue, since courage is valuable precisely in order to fight the evils of the human condition.

For Augustine, human virtue is promoted within a broader context of evil. As such, its value is like that of competent seafaring, when navigating against the rage of the much larger sea. Virtue does not liberate itself from

10. This position depends on his understanding of original sin. Even though human beings fell voluntarily, they are not strong enough to reach salvation by human effort and will alone. See *On Free Choice of the Will* 2.20.

11. As explained more fully below, Augustine argues that what the soul ultimately desires is the eternal well-being that only God's grace can provide. See his discussion in *The City of God* 19.4.

12. This war, again, implies that one does what one does not will. Augustine quotes the Apostle Paul in this regard (Gal 5:17). See *The City of God* 19.4.

vice, but rather lives always within a context of vice, within and among human beings.[13] He criticizes especially Stoic philosophers who emphasized Socratic autonomy and self-control to the extreme, who maintained that virtue and happiness are completely under human control regardless of circumstances.

Even if proper habituation would be sufficient for the attainment of virtue, it is plain that the vast majority of societies are not organized to educate their citizens in virtue. Rather, the qualities stressed are those that lead to victory over others, to material and worldly success. Most societies gratify appetites and the desire for domination, at the expense of reason. This was even true in Athens, the cradle of philosophy.[14] Accordingly, for Augustine the love of wisdom identified by Plato and Aristotle is sound in its desire (since the soul would be fulfilled by genuine virtue) but frustrating in terms of its strength. For human beings through their own efforts do not have the strength to live the life of virtue and philosophy, even if this life is understood as the continual cultivation of these ideals. The will's self-assertion, the evils mixed with and surrounding virtue, and the societies in which we are habituated prevent human beings from reaching by themselves, even temporarily, the restful peace and wholeness of genuine virtue.

II.1b
The Insufficiency of Speculative Philosophy

In terms of knowledge, Augustine does recognize that reason can discover the superior realm that illuminates the soul. However, the weakness of human nature regarding knowledge is similar to its weakness regarding virtue. The soul can discover the eternal forms and patterns that illuminate its vision, including God as the source of all truth, but lacks the strength to persist in the contemplation of these eternal things.[15] As the Platonists know, there is a hierarchy of truth, from sensible objects to the Good. The resources of Platonic philosophy were invaluable to Augustine, as he overcame skepticism and Manichaean dualism (which posited two conflicting and equally powerful principles of reality: good and evil).

---

13. See his discussion of the classical virtues in *The City of God* 19.4.

14. Adeimantus points out major deficiencies in Athenian (and generally Greek) moral education and tradition in book 2 of Plato's *Republic*.

15. See *Confessions* 7.17.

In terms of knowledge, Augustine sought for a sure foundation for truth, and he found this in Platonism. Platonic philosophy was, to Augustine, the proper employment of reason. Indeed, reason can demonstrate certain unshakeable truths and so overcome skepticism and relativism. Moreover, reason can discover a hierarchy of knowledge that is governed by truth, which is superior to the soul.[16] However, although human reason in inherently sound insofar as it relies on and recognizes the truth, it is not strong enough to reach what it most desires: abiding in the eternal truth.

Augustine begins to lay a foundation for truth in a way that foreshadows Descartes and modern philosophy, namely, through the certainty of the self's own existence.[17] I may be in doubt of everything, but not of my own existence, since I must exist in order to doubt in the first place. Hence, one may be sure not only of one's existence but also of the fact that one knows and lives as well. For one is aware of the knowledge of one's existence, and in order to know, one also must live. Moreover, knowing is higher than mere life, since knowing presupposes living, yet some living things do not possess knowledge. The same may be said about life compared to mere existence: living is higher than mere existence, since living presupposes existing, yet lifeless things also exist.

In terms of knowledge, which is above life and existence, there is also a hierarchy. The five senses (sight, hearing, etc.) are higher than mere sensible matter, since the senses judge and interpret this brute matter. However, the senses, the soul's doors to the external world, report to a higher faculty that is internal to the soul. This is the common or internal sense, the faculty (possessed also by nonrational animals) that organizes the information from the separate senses. For the eye cannot hear, the ear cannot see, etc. However, beasts and human beings know, when sensing a visible object that also emits sound, that the sound and the sight belong to the same object. This knowledge cannot be provided by the separate senses, but only by a faculty that judges and connects the separate senses. Hence, the common sense coordinates the information from the different senses in order to provide an organized experience of the beings of the sensible world (going beyond the disparate data given by the separate senses). Moreover, this common sense commands the five senses. For instance, when seeing

16. Augustine's hierarchy of knowledge is well developed in *On Free Choice of the Will* 2.3–15.

17. However, the spirit and method of Augustine's search for certainty are very different from those of Descartes, as will be shown in the next chapter.

an object that is emitting a soft sound, the common or internal sense commands hearing to pay closer attention. Thus, the common or internal sense interprets, coordinates, and commands the five senses.

Although beasts also possess an internal sense, they do not possess reason, the faculty by which human beings understand universal concepts (formulated in language) and make judgments and inferences. Reason classifies the different objects experienced through the common sense, communicates them in language, and judges their natures and attributes as well as the relations among them. In other words, reason judges and interprets the common sense, just as the common sense judges and interprets the five senses, and the five senses judge and interpret sensible matter.

Is there something higher than reason? First, reason sometimes errs, as we all know from experience. In these cases, reason recognizes its previous error and adopts what it later recognizes as truth. One may have made a mistake in mathematical calculation, even though mathematical truths are universally valid. These truths, once discovered and learned, are undeniable and are recognized as true for anyone, anytime, anywhere. Moreover, these truths are not the property of any one mind, since they are true for every mind that understands them, even though some minds can fail to understand them. In other words, reason does not judge truth as it judges the common sense. Rather, reason recognizes truth and submits to it when reason understands truth. Truth, which is fixed and universal, is higher than reason, since reason can change and err. Reason judges by truth, but it does not judge truth. Accordingly, truth is higher than reason.

In judgment, reason discovers to some extent the presence of what is eternal, immaterial, and divine. For in recognizing particular truths—in saying that three and seven make ten, in recognizing that this is better than that, etc.—reason appeals to unchanging, superior standards. When reason judges by the truth, reason can discover what is superior to reason, what governs and illuminates reason. All the different truths that reason recognizes share something essential, namely, the truth by which they are all true. The different truths are different insofar as they pertain to different aspects of knowledge, but not insofar as they are all true. That is why these different truths are all universal, unchanging, and necessary—the properties of truth. In other words, reason recognizes truths by truth itself, which is higher than particular truths, since particular truths share in truth itself, which extends beyond them. This Truth, the one source of all truths, is the source of universality, immutability, and necessity, as well the ultimate source of all things, since all things possess truth to the extent that they possess being. In other words, the Truth is the one and ultimate principle of reality. The Truth is equivalent to God.

According to Plato, just as equal things depend on equality itself, equality itself and all the other forms, precisely as forms, depend on the principle that gives them formal being and makes them intelligible objects (which possess unity, immateriality, eternity, etc.). Plato calls the first principle the Good because it gives of itself, because it gives being to all forms and, thereby, to everything else that participates in the forms. Plotinus speaks of the same principle, but his preferred term for it is the One, since this principle is also the transcendent Unity that is the source of all formal unities and, thereby, of all sensible things. Augustine, on the other hand, stresses the first principle's property of truth. Truth itself is the divine principle of all things, the source of being, as well as the superior wisdom that governs the realm of truths, which governs reason, which in turn governs the rest of the soul. This superior being is the very source and light of the mind's vision, since it is what the mind appeals to in recognizing truth, goodness, etc.

However, as the eye sees by means of light but cannot see the light itself by which it sees, the mind has serious difficulty learning about the superior source of its own intellectual vision. In a heartfelt passage of his *Confessions* (book 7, section 17), Augustine describes his first encounter with this superior realm, as he reflected on the source of his judgments. Through a flash of insight, in a brief and weak trembling glance, Augustine gathered all his spiritual strength to hold his intellectual sight toward this superior realm. However, all his efforts do not supply more than a mere spark of indirect vision. Quickly, his mind was pulled down by the realm below, by the house of sense and worldly custom in which the soul presently dwells. His conclusion is that human reason cannot persist, through its own efforts, even in the first stage of contemplation of divine truth. Reason, when properly used, points us in the right direction, but reason on its own is self-defeating in its efforts to reach its goal.[18]

18. To illustrate the impossibility of perfect knowledge of God in this life, various thinkers of the theological tradition have alluded to Exodus 33:20, which states that no one can see God face to face and live.

II.1c
The Drive for Synthesis

Augustine's love of wisdom, like ancient Greek love of wisdom, recognizes virtue and knowledge (truth) as the ends of the soul. However, Augustine is original in his own experience, expression, and interpretation of this love that stems from the core of the soul. Human love of wisdom has two faces. On the one hand, its direction is sound. On the other hand, its ultimate lesson is its fundamental weakness. Considered by itself, human love of wisdom is tragic. However, considered as a step toward faith, love of wisdom may be redeemed.

Before Augustine's intimate experience with philosophy as love of wisdom, he had serious misgivings about Christian revelation and could not accept its teachings, primarily because his original approach to these texts had been a literal one, whereby he had seen various (apparent) contradictions. However, he gradually learned to appreciate the wisdom of scripture, which speaks at many levels and in various senses about the most important subjects, so that its lessons become accessible to everyone.[19] His discovery and understanding of philosophy, as a basic calling of the soul that nevertheless cannot reach its goal unaided, opened the path of faith for him.

Although this path of faith is much more than pure philosophy, much more than the cultivation of virtue and knowledge according to human natural capacity, this path does use philosophy, but in an adapted form. What the soul ultimately thirsts for is God himself, but God and the path towards him are only insufficiently indicated by unaided philosophy. Human nature desires a goal that exceeds its own capacities, so that, considered purely in human terms, this desire is vain and futile. However, the recognition of this weakness and of the superiority of divine wisdom gives meaning to the human condition. For the very transcendence of the divine goal implies our inability to comprehend it fully, which at the same time justifies and encourages faith in God's superior wisdom (revealed in the scriptures), as well as hope for his healing grace. In the light of faith and revelation, one finds the real meaning of the insufficiency of human nature. In this light, humanity is part of creation. Human beings are, fundamentally, creatures. Accordingly, they both desire and need their Creator, even when they are

---

19. Ambrose was an important influence in this regard, as mentioned in *Confessions* 6.4–5.

not aware of this explicitly. In order to live well in this life, and in order to reach their ultimate purpose—salvation or eternal life—human beings need divine assistance. As creatures, they manifest their Creator at their very core. Therefore they can be understood adequately only in light of their Creator, which requires the wisdom of revelation. Faith in God and adherence to his revelation are necessary for virtuous living and essential for understanding created reality. Virtue and knowledge, the two chief and original goals of philosophy, need the strength and guidance of faith.[20]

Augustine therefore embodies love of wisdom in a new way. He is a lover of wisdom with his entire self (like Socrates, Plato, and Aristotle), with the added dimension of faith in the revelation that was not accessible to the ancient Greek philosophers. He recognized that the chief lesson of philosophy is its cry for help. Only through faith in God's grace can the soul hope to fulfill its core desire for virtue and knowledge, for the integration and completion of the soul. For this fulfillment depends ultimately not on human efforts, but rather on the gift of salvation. At the same time, the soul should prepare itself in this life for the next life, through holy living according to the way of Christ. The more the soul searches for the presence of God in all things (especially within the soul itself), the more the soul becomes free from material attachments and worldly custom. Holy living and prayer strengthen the soul's virtue and knowledge. The more pure a soul is, the more it is able to remain mindful of the illuminating and divine source of its judgments. The soul approaches God, who is the Truth, to the extent that it can rise above the material realm and discern the immaterial source of its knowledge. Spiritual living strengthens the soul both morally and intellectually. It purifies the character and polishes the intellect.[21]

In this Christian path, the resources of reason and philosophy do have an important place. After all, reason is grounded in divine illumination, as Plato had understood even without revelation. Without this revelation, however, Plato could not discern the full significance of reason and philosophy, the deeper levels in which creatures manifest their Creator. In other words, rather than suppressing philosophy, faith helps philosophy reach new heights. In the light of faith, Augustine develops (Platonic) philosophy into an expression of Christian wisdom, whereby reason both clarifies faith and is purified by faith. Faith strengthens reason, although of course never

20. See *Confessions* 7.18–21.

21. A classical expression of this approach is St. Bonaventure's *Journey of the Mind to God*, whose primary inspiration is Augustine.

to the point that reason could supplant faith and prove everything that is believed. The inherent and original weakness of reason—a human faculty aiming for what exceeds it—remains.

Yet reason can work with faith to find deeper insights than would otherwise be available. For instance, revealed data on original sin supplements philosophy. Philosophy does indicate the core desires of the soul, but scripture sheds light on the ultimate significance of these desires: the soul desires union with God but cannot reach him solely through its own efforts due to its presently wounded state, on account of original sin. Faith and grace are necessary for the soul to be healed and to reach its goal. In light of revelation, which stresses the absolute power and wisdom of the One God, Augustine also reinterprets the Platonic forms and incorporates them within a monotheistic vision: the forms should not be understood as various independent, necessary, and eternal principles (a form of polytheism),[22] but rather as ideas in the mind of God. The forms have reality, and the sensible world does reflect them, because they are found in God's knowledge, in God's creative art.

Augustine draws on philosophy and scripture to elucidate other articles of faith, such as the creation of the world, God's triune nature, and the teaching that the soul is made in the image of God. These matters, about which revelation speaks, exceed the capacity of reason alone, but with the help of faith reason can gain some understanding of them. Love of wisdom is no longer the cultivation of the character and the intellect purely according to what is naturally available, as Socrates, Plato, and Aristotle had assumed. True love of wisdom is love of the God of revelation with the whole soul, whose expression is adherence to Christ's way, since this is the path toward ultimate fulfillment (eternal life). In the case of those with the vocation for rational investigation, this love of wisdom does indeed employ the resources that the Greek philosophers also employed, but with an added dimension that transforms the very meaning of these traditional resources. According to Augustine, the lover of wisdom, who is also a philosopher in the traditional sense, uses the scriptures to orient his reason and reason to interpret the scriptures. True wisdom discerns in created reality the

22. Even though Plato clearly traces all the forms to one first principle, the Good, Plato's own view of the status of the forms themselves and their interrelation is still a source of debate. However, in the tradition it was not uncommon to interpret Plato as holding that the forms were independent substances. See Thomas Aquinas' reply in *Summa Theologica*, I, q. 84, art. 5. What is clear is Augustine's reformulation of the forms in the light of revelation (see *Eighty-Three Different Questions*, q. 46), as Aquinas also indicates.

presence of the Creator, as well as the way toward him.[23] This project is not possible through reason alone, which is too weak. A genuinely Christian way of life is essential in the search for wisdom.

In this life, faith supplements our weakness through meaning, guidance, and hope. Faith gives meaning to human natural desire, which is vain taken on its own. Faith provides guidance through a code of virtuous conduct accessible to everyone, not just philosophers. Specifically regarding philosophical knowledge, faith uplifts our vision, so that reality may be seen in light of the God of revelation. Faith strengthens us in this life (though without removing our weakness completely), primarily by nourishing hope for eternal happiness in the next life.

II.1d
Love of Wisdom as Love of the God of Revelation

The final expression of Augustine's love of wisdom is indeed rooted in human nature and desire. Like the Greek philosophers, his fundamental desires are for virtue and knowledge, for self-integration and truth. Also like these philosophers, Augustine sees the fulfillment of the soul in terms of assimilation to the divine. However, Augustine's love of wisdom is distinct insofar as his assessment of human nature, based on Platonic philosophy and Christian revelation, is distinct. Human beings are fundamentally creatures who desire their Creator. In order to reach its goal, human nature needs God's saving grace, which ultimately depends, not on human achievement, but on God's will. However, both philosophy and the scriptures call us to live righteously. Genuine human excellence lies in the proper channeling of human nature toward its supernatural goal. In this life, proper self-cultivation draws from what is naturally available to human beings and directs this toward God, who has the power to lift us toward him beyond our own capacities, even in this life. For example, the classical virtues (temperance, justice, courage, and wisdom) can lead to the infused or theological virtues of faith, hope, and charity. Similarly, worldly philosophy can lead to theological wisdom, to the comprehensive vision of being in light of revealed truth.

Irrespective of one's use of philosophy, everyone is a lover of wisdom, since everyone seeks happiness and only God can satisfy us fully. Christ has

---

23. This approach is evident in Augustine's reflections on the Trinity and on creatures as made in the image of the Trinity, a central mystery of the Christian faith.

opened the path for everyone. For those with a specific vocation for rational investigation, for those lovers of wisdom in the more narrow sense of the word, like Augustine himself, Christ has also illuminated the way, since revelation elevates philosophy, in terms of both virtue and knowledge.

Augustine's love of wisdom, like ancient Greek love of wisdom, is a complete love, in which the soul harnesses all of its aspects in seeking the divine. However, in the case of Augustine, love of wisdom is love of the God of revelation, which implies not only drawing from the soul but also the soul's trust in its Creator. Faith, in addition to reason, will, emotion, and appetites, becomes essential to love of wisdom. Faith redeems and nourishes love of wisdom, since faith establishes this love in the path that makes its goal possible.

II.2
MEDIEVAL ARISTOTELIAN LOVE OF WISDOM:
THOMAS AQUINAS

It is true that Aquinas departs from several important principles held by Augustine. After all, Aquinas saw in Aristotle, rather than in Plato, the better employment of reason, the better philosophical principles. However, like Augustine, Aquinas sees human nature as seeking an end that exceeds its capacity, and therefore as needing the help of revelation and faith. For Aquinas, as for Augustine, revelation is the ultimate authority. Revelation comes from God himself and speaks of matters that exceed reason. Revelation is indispensable and universal, since it makes the path toward salvation available to everyone, irrespective of philosophical instruction. In terms of his commitment to synthesize faith and reason into a Christian vision, Aquinas continues Augustine's work.

II.2a
Aquinas' Own Drive for Synthesis

Aquinas departs from Augustine in terms of the way in which he synthesizes faith and reason.[24] A fundamental difference between Augustine and Aquinas can be traced back to that fundamental difference between Plato and Aristotle: the former understands human knowledge in terms of recol-

24. See also Flores, "The Intersection of Philosophy and Theology," sections I-II.

lection and the latter in terms of abstraction. For Plato, we grasp the nature of things in the light of their eternal forms. As shown, Augustine develops this insight: God is the Truth that illuminates the mind, the Truth by which the mind grasps any truth. For Plato and Augustine, in intellectual vision the eternal realm makes itself present to the soul, which knows temporal things by comparing them to their eternal source, though without seeing this source openly (as explained). In this Platonic perspective, the chief error of reason is idolatry: taking material, temporal reality as the only true reality, that is, taking the copy for the original. Hence, Plato urges us to train ourselves to see with the mind's eye, to seek the immaterial forms themselves. Philosophy is the activity that lifts the soul towards the eternal realm, the realm of true reality to which the soul is by nature akin. As discussed, Augustine sees both soundness and futility in this philosophical program, since unaided reason cannot reach its goal. God's revelation and grace are necessary.

Thomas Aquinas, like virtually all medieval Christian thinkers, adopts Augustine's interpretation of the Platonic forms: the forms are God's ideas, God's creative art. The Platonic forms do exist, but only in God's mind. However, for Aquinas the forms of creatures themselves should be understood in the Aristotelian sense. As a Christian, Aquinas does believe in the creation of the world. However, regardless of whether the world is created or eternal (a question that Aquinas thinks reason alone cannot determine[25]), for Aquinas the sound doctrine on forms is that they are the immanent principles of the natural world, rather than separate causes. For change and motion can be explained only by the immanent causes that govern the different natural processes.[26] How can what is separate from motion, and itself motionless (namely, separate forms), influence changing things? Since the forms of things are in things, knowledge of these forms takes place by intellectually abstracting them from matter, rather than by comparing material things to their eternal exemplars. Accordingly, Aquinas rejects the view that knowledge depends on divine illumination.

Moreover, the human soul is itself the form of the body, the principle governing human development and activity.[27] Hence, in terms of knowledge, the basic affinity is between the soul and the forms of natural things,

---

25. See *Summa Theologica*, I, q. 46, art. 2. In this regard, Aquinas' position is influenced by the Jewish philosopher Moses Maimonides.

26. See *Summa Theologica*, I, q. 84, art. 1.

27. See ibid., I, q. 75, art. 1.

rather than between the soul and separate, eternal forms. As Aquinas puts it, the proper object of the human intellect is the quiddity or essence of a material thing,[28] which the intellect abstracts from material conditions. The forms, including the soul that knows the forms, are immanent principles.

The natural world, even if created, can be understood on its own terms, since its principles are immanent. Knowledge is also a natural process governed by immanent principles, and is not conditioned by the presence of God from above, so to speak. Surely, God is present in all knowledge, since everything ultimately comes from God, the first cause. Human knowledge approaches God, insofar as we reason from effects to causes, but not insofar as the presence of God illuminates the act of knowledge itself.[29] This position implies a different cooperation between faith and reason than the one conceived by Augustine, as well as a different conception of the way in which creatures manifest the Creator.

For Aquinas, faith begins where reason ends. Faith and reason are separate domains, separate sources of truth. In a sense, this is true in the case of Augustine and other medieval thinkers who follow Augustine's basic principles. Augustine does distinguish between faith and reason. After all, Plato pursued philosophy without revelation. On the other hand, one can approach the scriptures without using Greek philosophy, and they still offer the necessary guidelines for living rightly, as well as sound doctrine about God. However, for Augustine Christian wisdom blends faith and reason, since faith elevates, purifies, and strengthens reason itself. In this regard, faith and reason are not discrete domains according to Augustine. Since philosophy is grounded in God's illumination in the first place, faith in revelation is a real and necessary asset to philosophy itself.

On the other hand, Aquinas' Aristotelian principles lead him to conceive of the cooperation between faith and reason differently. Human knowledge proceeds from sensation to wisdom, which is knowledge of first causes. However, human knowledge remains tied to the sensible world: the first cause is known only through the effects we experience. Reason gathers that all changes and processes depend ultimately on a cause that is itself changeless, eternal and purely actual. However, reason only knows about this cause what it is not, namely, that it does not possess any of the attributes associated with the changing, sensible world. Hence, one may say that

28. See ibid., I, q. 85, art. 1

29. However, there is a sense in which illumination occupies a place in Aquinas' thought, as shall be explained below.

78

the first cause is not material, not mutable, not limited, not temporal, etc. Human beings, who by nature desire to know, remain dissatisfied with the fruits of unaided reason. For reason by itself can arrive only at the knowledge *that* God exists, but is unable to discover *what* God is.[30] Reason is too weak to understand the essence of the first cause, namely, God himself. Revelation, on the other hand, can supply in this life some of what reason lacks and inform humanity about the triune God and his plan for creation. Revelation not only supplements reason. It is also irreplaceable by human philosophy, since revelation provides everyone, regardless of instruction, with the necessary guidelines to reach salvation, the ultimate goal of the human soul.

The lover of wisdom should welcome revelation, which provides a wisdom exceeding human wisdom. The true lover of wisdom, who is aware of the limits of reason, should study not only the philosophical sciences (the sciences grounded in reason) but also theology (the science grounded in revealed divine wisdom).[31] Theology, based on a superior wisdom, is the highest science. At the same time, the theologian uses reason in his interpretation of the scriptures; that is why the theologian should also know philosophy. However, even though for Aquinas the lover of wisdom relies on both reason and revelation, philosophy and theology remain separate domains. Philosophy is grounded on the evidence of reason, while theology is grounded in faith, even if the theologian employs reason, since the premises of theology are still taken on faith.

As Aquinas puts it, philosophy and theology are *formally distinct.* Philosophy sees reality in light of the evidence of unassisted reason, while theology sees reality in light of faith and revelation.[32] Philosophy and theology discern distinct (but not contradictory) aspects of reality, just as the eye and the ear discern distinct aspects of the sensible world. Each source of truth is legitimate in its own right, even though revealed divine wisdom is superior to human wisdom. The conclusions about the world and its causes, based on sound reason, are legitimate. However, part of the evidence of reason is its own limitation (Aristotle also recognized this). Reason infers some of the ultimate causes but lacks the strength to understand them adequately. Accordingly, reason remains dissatisfied, if it relies purely on its own capacity. Revelation supplies some of the knowledge that reason lacks in this

---

30. See *Summa Theologica*, I, q. 2, art. 2.

31. See ibid., I, q. 1, art. 1.

32. See ibid., I, q. 1, art. 3.

life regarding the ultimate questions, so that human beings can prepare themselves for the next life. In this life, faith supplements reason, but the real satisfaction of reason, the open vision of the ultimate truth, is only possible in the next life, when vision will supplant faith and the soul's core desire to know will at last reach true fulfillment.[33]

Aquinas, in this way, finds solid principles in Aristotle, but also recognizes the ultimate weakness of pure philosophy. Only the Christian path can bring the basic human desire to know to its final goal. Yet philosophy's accomplishments, its conclusions about the nature of sensible things and about the existence of higher causes, are legitimate and adequate in their own domain, based on the evidence of reason. What reason lacks is not a better view of its very own domain. What reason lacks is knowledge about matters that exceed its own domain, about matters that are known only through revelation.

Divine assistance is central not only in order to obtain knowledge and intellectual virtue, but also regarding virtue of character. For living the Christian life, especially for those married to the church, can imply commitments that go beyond the basic dictates of reason alone (such as chastity, fasting, etc.), beyond the Greek understanding of the classical virtues (wisdom, justice, courage, and temperance). God's grace is necessary in order to cultivate the Christian virtues fully. That is why Aquinas and other medieval thinkers speak of the infused or theological virtues of faith, hope, and charity.[34] In this life, these virtues are the highest accomplishments of the intellect and character. Since these virtues are for the sake of God and the next life, which exceed human natural capacity, they require divine assistance. In this regard, both Aquinas and Augustine (regardless of their differences) consider revelation as the highest authority and place theology above purely rational philosophy.[35] According to them, the lover of wisdom in the complete sense loves the God of revelation with the entire soul. This love and calling of the soul, directed to an end that exceeds it, implies an openness and devotion to a transcendent authority, and therefore requires virtues that build upon purely natural virtue, namely, faith, hope and charity.

33. See ibid., II, q. 3, art. 8; q. 5, art. 5.

34. See *Summa Theologica*, I-II, q. 62, art. 1–3.

35. This attitude is not universally true in the Middle Ages, as shall be discussed below in relation to Avicenna and Averroes, two important predecessors of Thomas Aquinas.

II.2b
The Background of Aquinas' Conception of Wisdom:
Avicenna and Averroes

As discussed in the first chapter, Aristotle speaks of wisdom as the highest science, as the inquiry into first principles and causes. In this sense, wisdom is also called first philosophy. Wisdom may also be called theology, since the ultimate causes are divine. However, Aristotle also speaks of wisdom as the science of being as being, since wisdom is not a particular science but rather the most comprehensive and universal form of knowledge, which considers all beings precisely as being and investigates the principles and causes of being as such.[36] This science of being became more commonly known, in the history of philosophy, as metaphysics (literally: after or beyond physics), since this highest science is studied last, namely, after physics or natural philosophy. The name metaphysics is also associated with the fact that (traditional) metaphysics leads to the consideration of immaterial causes, of being(s) that transcend the physical world.

Aristotle's conception of metaphysics was a topic of intense discussion among his ancient and medieval students, who tried to develop this conception into a full-fledged science, beyond Aristotle's original, and often scattered, observations. Accordingly, several versions of Aristotelian wisdom developed prior to Aquinas' own time. Especially noteworthy among them are those by Jewish and Islamic thinkers who developed syntheses of religion and philosophy. Unlike their Jewish and Islamic predecessors, who possessed the texts of Aristotle by the ninth century, Christians scholars of western Europe only accessed Aristotle fully in the thirteenth century, when Latin translations of Aristotle's corpus (and many of its Jewish and Islamic commentaries) finally appeared. This background was a great asset to medieval Christian thinkers, who could learn from previous attempts at synthesis, even when they disagreed with their predecessors. Among these non-Christian thinkers, Avicenna (or Ibn Sina) and Averroes (or Ibn Rushd), two Muslims, are seminal.[37] They formulated two chief and competing versions of Aristotelian wisdom prior to Aquinas, who developed a third and equally influential version. Avicenna, also influenced by the Neoplatonic tradition, focused on wisdom as the inquiry into being as be-

36. See Aristotle, *Metaphysics* 4.1–2.

37. Basic accounts of the philosophies of Avicenna and Averroes are found in the entries devoted to them in Brown and Flores, *Historical Dictionary*.

ing, and in so doing paid particular attention to the existence of beings. Averroes, on the other hand, understood wisdom primarily as the rational inquiry into first causes, above all God. For Averroes, physics ends by accounting for motion through unmovable causes, while metaphysics deals with the unmovable causes themselves, especially the First.

Aquinas' conception of (Aristotelian) wisdom is based on his understanding of being as being, and to this extent Aquinas follows more in Avicenna's footsteps. Both Avicenna and Averroes considered rational knowledge as supreme knowledge, and they considered revelation (the Koran) largely as a popular expression of philosophy, whose chief value consists in guiding the masses in the path of righteousness.[38] For Averroes and Avicenna, reason and revelation agree. However, only the philosopher knows the deeper truths of scripture (such as those pertaining to God, creation, and the soul) scientifically or demonstratively. Still, the scriptures are irreplaceable by philosophy, since they, with their various senses and levels of interpretation, can reach everybody regardless of instruction. This general view of the relation between reason and revelation was not uncommon among medieval Islamic and Jewish thinkers. However, even though these thinkers saw philosophy as the highest form of knowledge, they themselves were not only philosophers. They were well versed in their scriptural traditions and laws, and active in their religious communities. To this extent, wisdom to them also included the religious life.

In medieval Europe (the Christian West), this was not the case. There, the theologian who also made use of philosophy was most associated with wisdom. Moreover, the medieval Christian figures who provided the most provocative treatments of philosophical questions were theologians first, such as Bonaventure, Thomas Aquinas, Henry of Ghent, John Duns Scotus, and William of Ockham. These thinkers, despite their differences, agreed in subordinating philosophy to theology, since theology deals with divine matters that exceed the capacity of pure reason, such as the Trinity and the Incarnation. To some extent, this contrast with the medieval Jewish and Islamic thinkers just mentioned has to do with the nature of Christian revelation itself, whose central tenets are properly called mysteries of faith. Even though the transcendence of God is stressed in Islam and Judaism,

---

38. One of the fathers of this view is the great Islamic thinker Al-Farabi, who influenced Avicenna, Averroes, and others within his own tradition, as well as several medieval Jewish philosophers.

these so-called mysteries are lacking. Moreover, Judaism and Islam, though they do emphasize faith, are primarily religions of law.

In the medieval Christian context, generally it is the theologian, not the pure philosopher, who considers the highest (revealed) truths.[39] In order to understand the nature and limits of human knowledge, and in order to teach and interpret the faith, this theologian also needs to draw from the wealth of philosophy. That is why, in the medieval Christian context, this type of theologian approaches wisdom more than the pure philosopher or the pure dialectician of scripture.

∽

As mentioned, Aquinas relies on Avicenna more than Averroes. Avicenna's chief metaphysical insight has to do with his interpretation of Aristotle's position that form gives being to matter, since form organizes matter. For Avicenna, Aristotle's account of being is incomplete, since form gives being to matter in the sense that it determines matter in a specific way, but form does not give being in the sense of existence. For a thing's essence, constituted by form and matter, does not necessarily imply existence. Rather, a thing's essence is in itself possible; it may exist or not exist. For example, the essence of a horse ("horseness") is defined and understood in the same way, regardless of whether the essence applies to a living or a dead horse, to an existing or a nonexisting horse. Hence, form only specifies a thing, but it does not give existence properly speaking. For Avicenna, existence is distinct from essence because another principle aside from essence is required in order to account for the very existence of things.

Avicenna's account traces all existence back to a first cause, the Creator who bestows and preserves existence. Essences are of themselves only possible. If they do exist, they cannot be the cause of their own existence. Moreover, the cause of existence cannot be the being that generates another being that shares its essence. For example, the parents of a living horse are not, properly speaking, the cause of the existence of this living horse. For the essence of the living horse is still only possible in itself, since the horse may cease to exist. Another principle is necessary to account for existence, as long as the being exists. In other words, to Avicenna the cause of existence must not only produce existence, but must also preserve existence as long as it lasts. In the case of the horse, its parents may die, while the horse

---

39. Not surprisingly, the greatest contributions in both philosophy and theology in the medieval universities came from theology faculties.

continues in existence. Accordingly, the parents only generate, but they do not cause existence in the proper sense of the word.

To Avicenna, Aristotle did not account for existence. He only accounted for how things exist, through causes that explain motion and change. Form determines how a thing exists, not the fact that it exists. The being that generates another of its own kind, or the artificer who makes an artifact, causes a motion or change, not existence itself. Accordingly, metaphysics, which considers the properties of being as being, deals primarily with existence and the causes of existence. In Avicenna's own account of the causes of existence, he formulates original doctrines concerning the relation between essence and existence, the nature of creation, and the attributes of the Creator. The fruits of his work earned him praise by some and condemnation by others. Among Muslims, some followed his philosophical investigation into traditional themes, like creation, while others considered his rationalizations impious. On the other hand, his greatest philosophical critic, Averroes, saw some of his central positions as erroneous, and his brand of Aristotelianism as a distortion of the original Aristotle, whose philosophy was for Averroes the summit of human achievement. In the Christian West, Aquinas and other important metaphysicians also disagreed with elements of Avicenna's philosophy. What is undeniable, however, is Avicenna's remarkable influence in the history of metaphysics. In the case of Thomas Aquinas, Henry of Ghent, and Duns Scotus, to name but a few, Avicenna was a starting point for their own reflections into being.

II.2c
Aquinas' Metaphysical Wisdom:
A Synthesis of Aristotle and Neoplatonism

Aquinas agrees with Avicenna's general position: the cause of existence cannot be form. A different cause that accounts for the very being of things is necessary. For, again, essence does not include existence. However, Aquinas' discussion of this issue develops along different lines.[40] Whereas Avicenna stresses the concepts of possibility and necessity—an essence is only possible in itself, so if the essence exists, this essence necessarily implies a relation to a cause that preserves it in existence for the duration of its existence—Aquinas stresses the concepts of potency and act. This difference

---

40. Aquinas's account is found in his treatise *On Being and Essence*.

is not only one of terminology. Whereas Avicenna conceives of existence as external to essence, as an attribute given to essence by a cause, Aquinas considers act as the last stage in the completion or perfection of essence.

To Aquinas, matter is in potency to form. Form perfects matter since form specifies and organizes matter. However, this union of form and matter does not suffice to account for actuality, since form only determines how matter has being, but does not provide actual being. Just as matter is in potency to form, essence (which includes form and matter) is in potency to act, and just as form perfects matter, act perfects essence. Accordingly, act is not an attribute external to essence, but rather is the completion of essence, the fruition of essence's potency.

Being, for Aquinas, means act first and foremost, since only actual being is full-fledged being. Everything that is contingent, though actual, owes its being, not as an attribute granted to a prior (possible) essence, but as the very perfection of its essence and nature. All existing things share in actuality, but only God is pure act, since only God is wholly unlimited. To this extent, namely, in terms of act, all things participate in God, and God is in all things, but not in any pantheistic sense, since pure act transcends all limitations.

All creatures have limitations. Material creatures have a twofold limitation. The first limitation concerns matter. Matter, the potential subject out of which form emerges, limits the form, since it restricts the form to be the form of the particular subject. The species or form of horses, for example, can be multiplied indefinitely, through the generation of horses by other horses. However, as possessed by a particular horse, the form is limited, since the form is individualized. A particular horse can develop as a horse only in a limited way, depending upon its particular qualities, abilities, and challenges—in a word, depending upon its given potentiality as a material subject. The second limitation concerns form or essence, since essence does not imply actuality. A cause of actuality, distinct from essence, is necessary. Just as matter is in potency to form, form together with matter are still in potency to act, which is the perfection of essence. Form, the principle that specifies a thing, limits act, since it restricts act as the act of an individual with a specific form. Matter limits form by individualizing it, while form limits act by specifying it (for instance, all that horses can be or do is still limited, by definition or essence, to only one realm of being, that of horses). An actual horse, therefore, entails a double composition as well as a double limitation. In terms of composition, there is a composition of form and matter, which composition is itself in composition with act. In terms of limitation, there is the limitation of form by matter, and the limitation of act by form.

All beings, except the first cause, owe their being, their actuality, since actuality does not stem from either matter or essence. All actual, material beings owe their actuality, since material essences (forms that exist in matter) do not contain actual existence inherently. Moreover, all actual, immaterial essences—beings that are both spiritual and one of a kind (since their essence is not individualized by matter or multiplied in many material subjects)—also owe their actuality for the same reason: their essences are distinct from act. These immaterial essences, intellects in Aristotelian terms[41] or angels in Christian terms, are still limited and caused. They are limited since their actuality is only that of their specific form. Their actuality is not subsistent or absolute.[42] They are caused, since they do not exist actually in virtue of their very essence. Their essence is not simply to be; rather, it is a specific mode of being that may be or not be. A cause of their actuality is required for them to exist actually in their specific mode of being.

The only being that does not owe its actuality is the same being that does not have any limitations. This is the first cause, which must exist since it is impossible for all beings to owe their actuality. Some cause, itself uncaused, must be ultimately responsible for the actuality of all things. Otherwise, every being would owe its actuality to another, which is impossible, since in that case nothing would exist actually, as there would be no original source of actuality. Since the first cause actually exists, its actuality must stem, not from another, but from itself, from its very essence. The essence of the first cause, unlike any other form, cannot be specified or be limiting in any way. Since the actuality of the first cause stems from itself, from its very essence, its essence is simply to be, rather than being in a certain way.[43] That is why this essence, unlike all other essences, which are caused, cannot be defined. This essence is pure act, subsistent act, act free of the limitations of matter and form, act free of any limitations whatsoever. Accordingly, the divine essence is infinite as well as transcendent.

---

41. In Aristotle's astronomy, these intellectual substances are the unmoved movers that are responsible for the uniform motion of the heavenly bodies. This was discussed in chapter 1, section I.3e.

42. See *On Being and Essence*, chapter 5.

43. See ibid.

Since it is the absolute plenitude of actuality, it contains, in a most eminent way, the perfections of all creatures. For in being pure act, this essence is also pure perfection, since act is the perfection of any being. For, to Aquinas, matter is in potency to form, while form is in potency to act.

Within this metaphysical framework, one may say that God is in all things and that all things participate in God, even though God is transcendent. For God sustains the being of all things, since God is act by essence, and the source of all actuality. On the other hand, in being actual, all things share in the divine reality through their own limited being, but without ever limiting or embodying this divine reality. In itself, the divine essence is wholly unrestricted actuality, and thus different in degree and in kind from any particular mode of actuality. This essence escapes all definition, measure and categorization, since, unlike all other essences, this essence is not a type of being but rather being simply, being in its full and unrestricted plenitude.

Accordingly, it cannot be grasped adequately by the human intellect.[44] This being can be described in negative terms, insofar as it is not like any creature, since it lacks all the limitations and imperfections of creatures. However, there is some discernible link between creatures and their Creator, since as pure act the Creator contains most eminently the perfections of creatures. In God these perfections are identical with pure actuality, having none of the limitations associated with creatures. Nevertheless, the limited perfections of creatures still manifest, though very indirectly, the unlimited perfection and actuality of the first cause.[45]

Moreover, one may repeat, though with an added Christian meaning, the Aristotelian position that all things approach the divine insofar as all things seek actualization. True, all things seek actualization according to their specific natures. However, unlike Aristotle, in Aquinas there is a sense in which the desire for actualization does go beyond the horizons of a thing's specific form. For in seeking actualization, a thing is also seeking the cause and source of its very being, God himself, who is subsistent act.

44. In other words, no concept or term can apply to God and creatures in exactly the same sense, or univocally. Interestingly, John Duns Scotus (d. 1308) will later criticize Aquinas and defend the univocity of the concept of being as applied to God and creatures. Of course, Scotus' understanding of being is different. Being is a quidditative concept in Scotus, a concept based on possibility rather than act.

45. On this basis, Aquinas criticizes the purely negative theology of Moses Maimonides and defends the analogy between God and creatures. See *Summa Theologica*, I, q. 13, art. 2 and 5.

This difference with Aristotle is not surprising, considering that in Aristotle form is the only principle of act, the principle that determines how a thing exists. Aquinas, on the other hand, stimulated by Avicenna and the Neoplatonic tradition, sees act as a principle distinct from form or essence, and sees act as caused ultimately by the first cause. In being actual, things manifest and participate in God, who is pure act.

Unlike traditional Platonic participation, Aquinas' version of participation stresses act more than form, since Aquinas adopts Aristotle's account of immanent forms. However, unlike Aristotle, Aquinas sees act as the perfection of form and, consequently, as the most significant dimension of beings, which most tellingly manifests the influence of the first cause on beings. Naturally, this participation in terms of act, in a sense, also includes form, since act is, in the case of limited beings, the perfection of form. At the core of their being, in their very actuality, things possess a divine spark, the sign of their cause and source. Moreover, in seeking preservation, development, and fulfillment according to their natures, things also (consciously or unconsciously) seek God himself, since God causes the act that is the fruition of their natures.

II.2d
Aquinas' Revised Aristotelian Love of Wisdom

Aquinas' metaphysical revision of Aristotle is also a revision of Aristotle's conception of love of wisdom as the core desire of the human soul. The specific human form is the intellectual soul, which organizes the human body and governs the development and activity of the human being. The activity that is proper to the human soul is understanding, since this is the activity that distinguishes human life from other life forms, as Aristotle rightly noted. Now, the intellectual soul is an immanent form, like other forms in matter, a form rooted in the potency of matter. Since human beings spring from the sensible world, the human soul belongs to this world and has a basic affinity with it (at all levels of life, namely nutrition, perception, and knowledge), as Aristotle also understood. This affinity is most telling in terms of human knowledge. Human beings by nature desire to know the world of their experience. Moreover, they are naturally equipped to do so, since the human intellect works by abstracting the forms of material things.

The deeper reality of the sensible world, its forms, patterns, and causes, is available to the intellect. The intellect, a spiritual reality that is nevertheless the form of the body, gathers what is intelligible—the universal forms—from particular, material things. The object, action, and nature of the intellect all correspond to each other in terms of form and matter: the intellect, the body's form (nature), by abstracting the intelligible form from the sensible images in the memory (action), knows the form of a material thing (object). In other words, the intellect is by nature suited to understand the forms of material things.

However, the intellect is more than its ability to abstract forms from matter. As already discussed in relation to Aristotle (in section I.3d), the intellect possesses two fundamental aspects. On the one hand, the intellect receives the universal forms unto itself. Knowledge is the identity between knower and known, whereby the intellect becomes the form of what it knows. In this regard, the intellect is a potential principle (the so-called possible intellect), which can become, and thus know, the different intelligible forms. On the other hand, the intellect is an active principle (the so-called active intellect) that actualizes understanding. For individual material things are actually sensible, but only potentially intelligible, since only universals are actually intelligible.

In the case of sensation, the sensible object is the active principle, since the object acts upon the organ to produce sensation, as when noise hits the ear and the hearing is activated. However, sensible objects, as individual, do not suffice to produce understanding. In the case of understanding, the intellect serves as the active principle, since the intellect extracts universals from individuals, making what is only potentially intelligible actually intelligible. This aspect of the intellect must be always active; without this prior active principle, the intellect could not move from potential to actual understanding. Aristotle likens this principle to light: light makes colors actually visible, while the active intellect makes universals actually intelligible. This principle, as the necessary and prior condition for any act of understanding, is by nature activity and is, accordingly, immortal.

The intellect defines the human soul. All things participate in and manifest the divine act through their own being. However, the human soul does so in a special way—in an intellectual way, in a way that approximates the divine reality more than other earthly beings. For God is not material. Rather, God is intellectual—supreme wisdom. Hence, Aquinas says that the intellect is a participation of the divine light. The intellect makes the vision of understanding possible. The intellect, the human form (which, like all forms, owes its being to the first cause), actualizes forms insofar as they become intelligible to us, analogously to how God is the ultimate cause of all actuality (and, thereby, also of all understanding).

In this sense, Augustine is right in saying we see things in light of their eternal exemplars, for we see the forms of things in the light of the intellect, which is a participation of the divine light. Yet this illumination does not take place by comparing the created to the uncreated form, but by participating in God through our own being and actuality, through our own specific form, the intellectual soul. Moreover, the actuality of the intellect also reflects the pure actuality of God in a special way, since the (active) intellect is subsistent.

Finally, the goal of the intellectual soul is actualization in knowledge. In virtue of the active intellect, the intellectual soul is already an actuality. As noted, in virtue of its actuality, the soul participates in and reflects the divine act. However, the soul also participates in and reflects the divine act in terms of its desire, in terms of its love of wisdom. For, over and above its basic reality as an active principle, as the prior light that illuminates all understanding, the intellect desires actuality in a subsequent sense. For the intellect desires to actualize its potency, desires its own development as possible intellect, through the acquisition of knowledge. This desire for self-development, for actualization or perfection according to form, is, ultimately, the desire to approach God, who contains most eminently the perfection of all forms in virtue of being pure act.

The intellect has an affinity to the sensible world, insofar as sensible reality can be understood formally and universally. However, of itself, the intellect relates and is akin to whatever is intelligible, including things that are not sensible at all. That is why Aquinas notes that, even though the proper object of the intellect is the quiddity of a material thing, the general object of the intellect is being.[46] For anything that has being is intelligible, and potentially known by the intellect. In this life, due to the limitations of the body and the material world, the intellect is not able to reach its full potential. Since knowledge begins and is grounded in the abstraction of forms from sensible things, which are effects, human knowledge proceeds from effects to causes. The highest accomplishment of (unassisted) reason is the knowledge of the first cause, not on its own terms, but through what the effects reveal about this cause. Yet, of itself, the intellect remains open to the fullness of understanding proper to the next life.

---

46. See *Summa Theologica*, I, q. 78, art. 1.

The intellect's desire to know is not satisfied in the knowledge of material things themselves, but only in the knowledge of first causes, above all God. Moreover, the most satisfying knowledge would be, not merely the knowledge of God through his effects, but the knowledge of God himself, the knowledge of his essence. The fulfillment of the human soul, the intellectual soul, lies in the attainment of the goal that is proper to its nature, namely, knowledge in its most complete form. This is the soul's own expression of the desire for actualization that is common to all things. For the intellect grows, actualizes its own potentiality, through the acquisition of knowledge. The consummation of this potentiality would be the open vision of the essence of the first cause, the reason by which everything is and is known. True, the intellectual soul, like all forms, is an immanent form. Yet, all immanent forms also participate in the Transcendent, in virtue of the act that perfects them as forms.

The human desire for actualization does extend beyond the horizons of its specific form, toward God himself, since the basic perfection of its specific form, namely, its actuality, is a participation in God who is pure act. Or, to put it in another way, the human desire for actualization does remain within the bounds of its specific form, but the very being of this specific form is its participation in the Pure Being that is its source and goal. Accordingly, the human desire for actualization, for perfection, is a tendency inscribed at the heart of a being that is, from the start, a participated being, and consequently the nature of this tendency is to approximate ever more adequately that divine source in which it participates. In other words, Aquinas has grounded the fundamental drive for actualization that Aristotle saw as defining all things in the prior, constitutive act that each being, as being, owes the first cause. Hence, for each being the desire for actualization is governed by the being's specific form, but the being itself, as already actual, is grounded in God. Therefore, actualization, as the fulfillment of a thing's potencies, is based on the prior and constitutive being of the thing as a participated act.[47]

47. The major medieval Jewish and Islamic Aristotelians (though not without adjustments) remain closer to Aristotle in this regard: they do not understand the impulse for actualization as stretching beyond the horizons of the specific form. This particular revision of Aristotle is more common in the Christian tradition. As suggested, this understanding is possible in Aquinas due to his own inclusion of the Platonic notion of participation within his metaphysics. Even though Aquinas conceives of philosophy and theology as separate domains, his Christian background, as is to be expected, did influence some of his philosophical interests and, consequently, some of his insights and discoveries, especially regarding metaphysical questions. In this case, Aquinas provides

The desire for perfection according to form is also the desire for God himself, since God is pure act and, thereby, the absolute perfection of all forms. In seeking self-development, beings, at their core, are seeking God, since God is their ground as well as their goal, their sustainer as well as their final accomplishment. Accordingly, in terms of love of wisdom, the goal is not only growth in knowledge or the possession of knowledge, but also necessarily union with God. That the soul seeks the highest knowledge means that it seeks God not merely as some separate object, but rather and more fundamentally assimilation to God himself, since God is the ultimate fulfillment and perfection of the human form.[48] Since this is the ultimate goal, which exceeds human capacity taken on its own, faith and revelation are essential in this life. Love of wisdom, insofar as it is ultimately a desire for God himself, cultivates reason and faith, for the sake of eternal life and the open vision of God, which is also the ultimate stage of human perfection and actualization.

II.3
THE CORE OF MEDIEVAL LOVE OF WISDOM

II.3a
The Common Core of Ancient and Medieval Love of Wisdom

Although Augustine and Aquinas develop their philosophies along different lines and conceive of the relation between reason and faith differently, there is a common core to their love of wisdom. One aspect of this common core is shared with the Greek philosophers, while another aspect is not. Like the Greek philosophers, Augustine and Aquinas see love of wisdom as a complete love, stemming from the whole soul and seeking complete

---

a metaphysical framework whereby creatures seek union with the Creator. Henry of Ghent, who develops the Platonic tradition of Augustine and Bonaventure, also uses Aristotle extensively and interprets the desire for actualization as aiming for union with God himself. A summary of other positions in the medieval tradition regarding this aspect of love of wisdom is found in section IV ("Love of Wisdom and Medieval Thought") in Flores, "Love of Wisdom," 631–33.

48. In this sense, it would not be illegitimate to associate some mystical elements with the thought of Aquinas. Naturally, these mystical elements are never as pronounced as those found in the writings of his fellow Dominican Meister Echkart, who also focuses on the intellect's connection with God.

fulfillment. Love of wisdom is ultimately the desire for happiness, and genuine happiness is found in virtue and knowledge, in the perfection of the soul and in the understanding of the highest truths, respectively. Happiness is also freedom—freedom from the bondage of vice and ignorance, whereby the soul lives deliberately and excellently.

II.3b
The Proper Core of Medieval Love of Wisdom

However, unlike the Greek philosophers, Augustine and Aquinas understand the ultimate significance of love of wisdom, its ultimate goal, and the means to its attainment in different terms. True, love of wisdom is desire for happiness rooted in the whole soul. However, the soul, which is made in the image of God, desires God himself, its source and end. Complete happiness is found only through union with God, through eternal life, which means that happiness is a goal beyond our limited nature. Our happiness depends, ultimately, on God's grace. In this life, we can contribute toward our goal through living wisely. However, in order to live wisely, in order to cultivate virtue and knowledge properly, it is essential to rely not only on the light of reason but also on the light of revelation. Revelation supplies us with the added wisdom and strength to prepare ourselves for the next life. It guides our characters and lifts our contemplation. In a word, revelation enhances that basic drive of the soul—the love of wisdom, whose significance the Greek philosophers only partially gathered—so that it is more worthy of its goal.

In spite of the differences between Augustine and Aquinas, and in spite of their extensive use and development of philosophy, both subordinate reason to revelation, philosophy to theology. For both see the fruition of love of wisdom as requiring divine assistance, and consequently both understand the pursuit of wisdom in terms of the synthesis of reason and faith. In this regard, they are not only exemplary of the general framework of medieval Christian thought. They are also two of its greatest sources. Even though this chapter for the most part limited itself to these two thinkers, the discussion sufficed to indicate the essence of medieval Christian love of wisdom in its two chief versions. For in the Christian tradition, the overwhelming majority of thinkers, some of whom produced highly original views, pursued wisdom in a spirit that can be associated either with Augustine or with Aquinas. Therefore, regarding the spirit of love of wisdom, namely in terms of the very drive of the soul for ultimate fulfillment, which is the focus of this book, the limited discussion in this chapter suffices.

∾

Having discussed chief ancient and medieval versions of love of wisdom, as well as the common core of this love among the ancients, the common core of this love among the medievals, and what is common among ancients and medievals, we now turn to the discussion of philosophical desire in light of modern philosophy. Against the background of the ancient and medieval traditions, in which love of wisdom shares basic roots despite its different versions, modern philosophy, as a form of desire, grounds itself on different vital sources. In the modern context, love of wisdom, as traditionally understood, is no longer the drive that fuels the activity of philosophers. Accordingly, in the modern period, one may speak of philosophical desire, but not of love of wisdom in the classical sense, in the sense proper to ancient and medieval philosophy. Alternatively, one could say that in the modern period, love of wisdom acquires a radically new meaning, and then one could proceed to clarify this new meaning of the term. However, for the sake of consistency, this book shall reserve the term "love of wisdom" to indicate the traditional sense common to ancient and medieval philosophy. On the other hand, broader terms, such as philosophical desire or philosophical love, will be used in reference to modern philosophers. Hence, this book sometimes speaks about classical philosophical desire (or love), but it does not speak about modern love of wisdom, since philosophical desire (or love) is the broader term that applies to all the thinkers included in this book, to the entire subject of this work.

The new, modern philosophical context, its developments and lessons as they bear upon the central topic of this book, will be the subject of the next chapter.

Chapter 3

The Modern Break—Disparate Philosophical Loves

As seen in the previous two chapters, in terms of love of wisdom there is significant continuity between ancient and medieval philosophy, at least among those major thinkers selected in this book. This is so despite the inherent differences and cultural contexts of these two periods, and despite the important differences among individual philosophers. Put simply, this continuity is based on a shared vital source and aim of love of wisdom. In ancient and medieval thought, love of wisdom is complete love, namely, the desire of the whole soul (character and intellect). Accordingly, its aim is also comprehensive: the fulfillment of the soul as a whole. Hence, ancient and medieval love of wisdom stresses virtue, understood as the best condition for the soul, as well as knowledge of the highest truths, the greatest fulfillment of the intellect. In a word, ancient and medieval love of wisdom seeks complete happiness. Naturally, this general principle assumes different forms, and is understood in varying terms, as it develops in the ancient and medieval traditions. Yet the principle remains.

The first step in coming to terms with modern philosophical desire is to recognize that modern philosophy is no longer grounded in the comprehensive drive characteristic of previous philosophy. Rather, modern philosophers manifest specialized or fragmented philosophical loves. Certainly, the revolutionary scientific, cultural, economic, and political changes that usher in the modern period influenced philosophical activity. Although these events may be quite relevant (and in the case of some thinkers more so than in the case of others), this work is not based on the assumption that historical contexts completely determine philosophical activity. Enough variety may be seen within a single historical time and place to reject this position. Rather, we will approach these authors on their own terms. We shall examine the philosophical drives found in major modern thinkers insofar as these drives produce philosophies. As was the case regarding the choice of ancient and medieval thinkers, the philosophers treated in this chapter were selected because they are outstanding representatives of the period, and because their examination complements the discussion of philosophical love.

III.1
DESCARTES' DRIVE FOR CERTAINTY

René Descartes (1596–1650) speaks of his own philosophical vocation in terms that remind us of the love of wisdom manifested by ancient and medieval thinkers. He claims that his dedication to the truth is, of all possible callings, the most satisfying, as well as the greatest asset for conducting his life well.[1] In associating his own philosophical pursuit with what satisfies in the extreme and with living well, Descartes would seem to love wisdom with his whole self, as something that provides complete and integrated fulfillment. Perhaps this was the case for Descartes personally. However, this classical sense of love of wisdom is not a determinative principle in his writings. Whereas ancients and medievals spoke of love of wisdom as seeking the highest fulfillment of the whole self, and actually focused much of their work on the various issues associated with happiness in the full sense, Descartes' own philosophy overwhelmingly stresses one aspect of the self and, consequently, one specific mode of satisfaction.

With Descartes, philosophical activity is no longer reflective of the basic yearnings that ultimately motivate all human activity. Rather, Cartesian philosophy is grounded in a specialized dimension of the human self, namely, in thinking insofar as it yields absolute certitude, and not on the whole soul as understood by previous thinkers. Accordingly, Cartesian philosophy, as a calling, is specialized in a sense that is very different from the sense in which ancient and medieval philosophy is a specialized calling. As we shall see in the next sections of this chapter, other modern philosophers

---

1. Descartes, *Discourse on Method*, Part 3, sections 27–28.

are also specialized like Descartes, although they ground their philosophies in different, albeit equally particularized, aspects of the human being.

For ancients and medievals, all human beings are lovers of wisdom, since all human beings seek complete fulfillment (even though some may pursue it in the wrong way), while lovers of wisdom in the narrow sense are those dedicated to this purpose in the highest way, through the cultivation of virtue and knowledge. In other words, for ancients and medievals, love of wisdom in the narrow sense is rooted in humanity's universal love of wisdom, and consequently rooted in human nature as a whole, since the former is the highest and best expression of the latter. Even though the ancient and medieval lovers of wisdom (in the narrow sense) represent the very few in their societies, they do not see themselves as pursuing a specialized activity that is divorced from the basic yearnings of human nature understood in its full complexity, which includes appetitive, emotive, and intellectual dimensions, soul and body, intellect and character.

On the contrary, their pursuit centers on bringing these basic yearnings to their highest fruition. Their pursuit differs from that of everyone else not in terms of its fundamental root, but only in terms of its mode of expression. Everyone's calling is to seek complete fulfillment, and love of wisdom (in the narrow sense) is the highest answer to this calling, even though not everyone possesses the necessary education, talents, and leisure to pursue wisdom in this sense. This highest calling is also essential for society, which needs leaders and teachers who know the best forms of organized living, those most conducive to virtue and genuine happiness. For those unable to pursue wisdom fully in the narrow sense, it is still possible to work towards happiness and the common good by cultivating their own excellences, by noble actions and habits, and by following just laws.

III.1a
The Exigencies of the Thinking Self

On the other hand, Descartes focuses on what he calls the thinking self, whose proper satisfaction consists in certainty. Whereas previous thinkers, in seeking the integration of the self, considered the body, appetites, and emotions, and their relation to the intellect, Descartes, in seeking the satisfaction of certainty, excludes what does not provide him with indubitable evidence. Whereas previous thinkers, in recognizing the inadequacy of human wisdom compared to divine wisdom, explored extensively the analogous and indirect ways in which the human mind can come to terms with divine reality, Descartes, even in his recognition of God's transcendence, focuses only on what is certain to him as a thinking thing. These are only a few examples to indicate that in terms of love of wisdom, in addition to many other aspects commonly associated with the father of modern philosophy, Descartes represents a real break.

Descartes' method is consistent with his general aim, which is to build a philosophy on a totally certain foundation, namely, on the self-evidence of thought. This philosophy cannot be based in any way on sources that are external to the thinking self, such as sensible objects, tradition, the opinions of others, or even the body, since these have been sources of deceit at some point or other. Through the senses, things often appear differently than they really are. The sun seems to the eye smaller than the earth, even though astronomers know it is much bigger. Ordinary sense experience also seems to indicate that the earth is stationary rather than in motion. As we know, even some of the most authoritative traditional assumptions have been rejected as false, let alone many of the opinions we encounter in daily life. Accordingly, it is safer to exclude these sources altogether, since there is no guarantee that what has deceived us, even if only once, will not do so again in the future. Rather, the safest route is to doubt everything that can be doubted, even when falsehood seems highly improbable.[2]

What is subject to doubt includes not only external things but also ourselves, to some extent, beginning with the body. After all, our convictions based on our bodily experience depend on the senses, and therefore can be deceitful. Many times, for example, the pain we feel does not indicate the place of our malady. Even though people seem fairly confident in distinguishing being awake from being asleep, the distinction is still doubtful, since when we dream we generally believe we are awake. Accordingly, even those convictions that seem quite probable (such as those based on repeated experience or common sense) should be doubted, since they can be doubted. The fact that they are probable is irrelevant if our goal is absolute certainty, since often in the past what has seemed highly probable (such as the earth's stationary position, the trustworthiness of a certain person, etc.) turns out to be false. The slightest cause for doubt is sufficient for complete doubt, when the goal is absolute certainty.

2. Meditation One, "Concerning Those Things That Can Be Called into Doubt," in *Meditations*.

Naturally, when we act we often have to rely on probabilities. However, the issue at hand concerns theoretical knowledge:[3] is there an unshakeable foundation for absolutely certain knowledge? Mathematical truths impose themselves on the mind that understands them with clear and distinct evidence. These truths seem true regardless of time, place, and circumstance. For Descartes, a distinguished mathematician, the goal is to develop a philosophy (including a scientific method) that is certain in the way that mathematics is certain. Surely, many people commit errors in mathematical calculation, even in very simple operations. In these cases, the error lies with the individuals who are not yet mathematically competent. These individual errors are not sufficient to doubt mathematical reasoning itself, which appears universally valid (when properly understood). The evidence of mathematical reasoning is compelling since it is recognized within the mind by the mind itself, without having to rely on external sources.

However, in the *Meditations*, while seeking a foundation for certain knowledge, Descartes subjects even mathematical reasoning to doubt. Interestingly, as shall be shown, he subjects mathematical reasoning to doubt in order to validate it, in order to certify its very foundation and, consequently, the certainty of its results. Can we trust mathematical intuition at all, even when it appears methodic and sound? Is it possible to err when I, say, add two and three, carefully counting, and my intuition tells me that the answer is five? Erring in this case seems impossible, since the answer is self-evident to the mind, which here operates according to so-called sound mathematical standards. Even when uncontaminated by sense and the external world, in complete abstraction from everything outside the reasoning mind itself, what guarantees the accuracy of the mind's own mathematical logic?

It is possible, Descartes points out, that the mind is manipulated by a higher entity, which makes the mind err, while the mind believes it hits the mark. This would have to be some type of evil genius, who deliberately deceives us through the workings of our very own minds, through our very selves.[4] However improbable this hypothesis might seem, what evidence do we possess to demonstrate its impossibility? Simply our trust in our own minds? If so, this is not enough to provide an absolute foundation for certainty. Descartes' methodical doubt, culminating in the hypothesis of the evil genius, is helpful in purging us from continuing to give undue credence

3. Ibid., section 22.
4. Ibid., section 21.

to our previously held opinions. These opinions are probable at best, but not certain. Again, the purpose of methodical doubt is not to curtail all bases for action, or for us to reject as false everything we previously only assumed (since assuming falsehood, like assuming truth, assumes a level of certainty that we do not possess). Rather, the purpose is to highlight the rigorous standards of genuine certainty, so that either a sure foundation for truth is found, or the impossibility of this goal is recognized. Without any demonstration to discard the hypothesis of the evil genius, the latter case seems more likely. In this sea of doubt, where the mind cannot even trust its own inner logic, no certainty at all seems possible, let alone the possibility to erect a sure philosophy. Yet, just as some marks are visible only when everything else is dark, if any certainty does exist, it will surface in this environment of doubt, precisely due to its basic contrast with it.

III.1b
The Self-Evidence of Thought

At this stage, however, one thing is certain. No matter how deceived one might be, the fact of one's existence is indubitable, for one must exist in order to be deceived in the first place. As Descartes puts it: I think, therefore I am.[5] As long as the activity of thinking takes place, the existence of the thinking self is certain. This activity of thinking includes not only reasoning, judging, and doubting but also willing, imagining, feeling, and sensing, since the mind is conscious and thinks about these phenomena.[6] In other words, physical, emotive, and appetitive content is considered here only as modes of thought: I think that I feel, I think that I sense, etc. The mind might be wrong about what it thinks, about any of the things it judges, feels, or senses, even about their existence. However, the very activity of the mind, and consequently its existence, is indubitable. Any action of the mind presupposes the existence of the thinking self. This much is certain.[7]

---

5. Meditation Two, section 25.

6. Ibid., section 28.

7. Like Augustine, Descartes grounds certainty on the thinking self. Descartes proceeds from this point of departure in a different direction, however. Augustine (as explained above, in section II.1b) reflects on the hierarchy and continuity of knowledge, from sense to truth, from what is below to what is above the mind. The soul relates to all levels of reality in Augustine; it is the microcosm. Descartes, on the other hand, highlights substantial boundaries between what is interior and exterior to the thinking self.

Against the dark background of methodic doubt, the existence of thought is the first, original certainty that imposes itself on the thinking self. It imposes itself because of its fundamental property, which distinguishes it from everything that can be doubted. This property is clarity and distinctness, which makes it indubitable. The existence of the thinking self is supremely evident, since it is self-evident in the highest sense: it is the evidence that thinking possesses about itself. The thinking self clearly and distinctly knows itself as a thinking thing, since the activity of thinking discloses that which thinks, insofar as it thinks. I think; I am.

However, concerning the self, only thinking is evident at this point. Everything outside thinking, such as the existence of the body, still can be doubted, since only the senses lead us to believe in the existence of the body and the outside world. That we sense, as thinking things, is evident. However, that our senses correspond to external reality in some way, or even that there is external reality, is still doubtful. It is still possible that an evil genius creates for us an illusory world. What is no longer possible is to be deceived about everything, since the existence of the thinking self is indubitable. Moreover, insofar as thinking becomes the ground of Descartes' philosophy of certainty, other dimensions of human experience fall outside the realm of truth and certainty, and outside the scope of Descartes' philosophical desire, which is after pure certainty.

In finding his first certainty, Descartes has also discovered the standard for certainty. If anything else, aside from the existence of the thinking self, is certain and cannot be doubted, it also must possess the property of clarity and distinctness. Conversely, if something is perceived clearly and distinctly, it must be true. Descartes is confident in positing this general principle. Yet, of what other truths can the mind be certain, if an evil genius still may deceive it about everything else? Even matters that seem very clear and very distinct, such as that three and two make five, become doubtful when we hypothesize a supreme power capable of deceiving the mind's inner logic. Without certainty of the impossibility of this hypothesis, everything can be doubted, except perhaps[8] the existence of the thinking self, since in order for thinking to be deceived in every other respect, thinking must exist in the first place.

In other words, the very first certainty in Descartes' philosophy is also unique, since the clarity and distinctness of this certainty is unequaled by

---

8. There are moments when the hypothesis of the evil genius seems to shake Descartes' confidence about any possible certainty. See Meditation Three, section 36.

any other candidate for certainty. That two and three make five, and other propositions of this sort, seems quite clear and distinct, but not so much as the existence of the thinking self, since these propositions are called into doubt by the hypothesis of the evil genius, while the existence of the thinking self seems to pass muster even in this case. However, Descartes' principle, that everything that is clear and distinct is certain, is ineffective if it applies in one case only, if it is not a *general* principle. In order to use clarity and distinctness as the criterion for certainty, Descartes needs to be able to trust the adequacy, not only the existence, of thinking, and to be able to trust thought in this way the hypothesis of the evil genius must be first discarded.

III.1c
Descartes' Procedure

Accordingly, at this point, Descartes decides to investigate the existence of God.[9] If the mind can discover that God exists, and that God is not a deceiver, this would not only constitute an additional and fundamental truth. Discarding the possibility of an evil genius would guarantee the certainty of the mind's conclusions, when these conclusions are perceived clearly and distinctly. In other words, Descartes needs to establish the existence of God as a nondeceiver in order to be certain even about what seem to be elementary truths, such as those of basic mathematics. The question that comes to mind about this procedure is the following. If, at this point, the mind is unsure about its adequacy in establishing the certainty of, say, the sum of three and two, what equips the mind to investigate with certainty the existence of a nondeceiving God, a seemingly much more difficult and complicated task? If the mind is unsure about its most basic integrity as a seeker of truth (aside from its capacity to know its own existence), any conclusion that this mind reaches about God would have to be uncertain, even if the conclusion seems clear and distinct. For the reliability of clarity and distinctness is the question in the first place.[10]

9. Meditation Three, section 36.

10. The reader will decide if Descartes' argument for the existence of God (analyzed below) addresses these questions. In this regard, an important point is Descartes' claim that the idea of God is in fact prior to all other ideas, including that which the thinking self has about itself. See below.

At any rate, one can at least appreciate the order of Descartes' procedure as far as it relates to his general intention. His first step is grounding his philosophy in the existence of the thinking self, the only sure entity. Every other feature commonly associated with the human self, such as the body, as well as all reality that is viewed as external to the thinking self, is uncertain and therefore excluded. His second step is justifying the use of clarity and distinctness as a general criterion for truth. This second step requires establishing the existence of a nondeceiving God. If this second step can be accomplished, the mind can rely on its own clear and distinct ideas, and the third step of Descartes' philosophy becomes possible: to establish truths about the rest of reality. Hence, Descartes' philosophy moves from the thinking self, to God, to the rest of reality. This procedure is the inverse of the general procedure of ancient and medieval philosophy, which begins with experience and ends with the divine—begins with what is easiest to know but has a low degree of reality, and ends with what is hardest to know but has the highest degree of reality.

This procedure is demanded by Descartes' urge to establish a sure foundation for a scientific method based on clear and distinct ideas, which ideas are manifest above all in the mathematical sciences. It is one thing to develop these sciences according to their own principles, as Descartes himself did through his brilliant mathematical contributions. It is another thing to ground the principles of these sciences in the certainty of the thinking mind. This latter, metaphysical task is the task of the *Meditations*, Descartes' foundational philosophical work. This work deserves special attention, since in this work Descartes discusses the basic roots and requirements for all genuine knowledge and illustrates his own desire for knowledge, which is the desire for certainty understood in terms of clarity and distinctness.

This is a specific desire that engages a specific dimension: the thinking self in its inner certitude. True, this desire is comprehensive in the sense that it seeks the ultimate truths. However, what it seeks about the ultimate truths, and about any truth, is a specific property, namely, clarity and distinctness, as these are the marks of certainty. This is not surprising, if we consider that Descartes' fundamental ambition was to universalize, through the criterion of clear and distinct ideas, the certitude of the mathematical sciences.[11] This requires establishing with certainty the fundamental source of all certainty, namely, ratifying the adequacy of clear and distinct ideas.

---

11. *Discourse on Method*, Part Two, sections 20–22.

III.1d
God as the Source of Certainty

Descartes bases his argument for the existence of God on the idea of God.[12] Of the various ideas of the thinking self, one is very special: the idea of an infinite and supremely perfect being, a being that lacks nothing. This idea is not the idea of a body, since bodies are understood as limited entities. Accordingly, this idea lacks sensible or imaginary content. Rather, this idea is understood by the thinking self through its own meaning, although the full significance of this idea is not entirely clear, precisely because the thinking self is aware of its own imperfections and, therefore, of the superiority of supreme perfection. However, Descartes argues, because this idea is unique in referring to absolute perfection, it is also unique in that it must refer to a real being. Other ideas do not necessarily correspond to real things, since the existence and nature of the external world is doubtful. However, just as the existence of the thinking self distinguished itself from everything that can be called into doubt, the idea of God distinguishes itself from all other ideas, since of all ideas the idea of God must correspond to a real entity distinct from the thinking self.

Descartes explores the possible sources of this idea. All that Descartes knows for sure at this point is his existence as a thinking thing. Yet he has many ideas. Some of these ideas seem to correspond to other entities, such as the various ideas about sensible objects. Others seem purely fictitious, such as those fabricated by the imagination, like the idea of a golden mountain or a flying horse, etc. Other ideas are innate, like the idea of himself as a thinking thing, since this idea is part of his essence as a thinking thing: thinking about anything presupposes that which thinks; to be clear about anything is to be all the more clear about that which clearly thinks.[13] However, those ideas regarding sensible things are not necessarily caused by the external world; the existence of this world is still doubtful. There exists the possibility that these ideas also could come from himself, if he has some faculty that produces them, a faculty with which he is not yet familiar.

These ideas concerning (a possible) external reality have different degrees of mental being, what Descartes calls "objective" being, the being

---

12. Descartes' argument that God exists and is not a deceiver is well developed in Meditation Three, sections 37–52. He also provides a second argument for God's existence in Meditation Five. We will focus on the more developed treatment of Meditation Three.

13. Why the mind is better known than the body is explained in Meditation Two.

they possess as objects of the mind. For example, the idea of a substance, such as the idea of a horse, possesses more objective being than the idea of one of its accidents, such as the color of the horse. If horses do exist, they as substances would have more actual being (or formal being, in Descartes' terms) than their accidents, since accidents inhere in and depend upon substances. Although some ideas may refer to nothing actual, ideas themselves are not nothing, and in fact differ in terms of the being they possess as ideas. Accordingly, ideas cannot come from nothing. They must have a cause, a cause that possesses at least as much reality as the effect. The effect cannot exceed the cause in terms of degree of reality. Otherwise, something (the being through which the effect exceeds the cause) would come from nothing, which is impossible.

After an examination of his various ideas, Descartes concludes that his own being as a thinking thing is sufficient to account for all of them, except the idea of God. The innate ideas are bound with the thinking self. Moreover, it is possible that he, a thinking substance aided by a faculty or faculties of which he is not fully cognizant, is able to generate all the ideas about the (possible) outside world. However, he cannot be the source of the idea of an infinite and supremely perfect being. Yet this idea must have a cause.

The idea of God must have God himself as its source. For the idea of God cannot come from an external, sensible world, if such a world exists, and it cannot come from the thinking self. The idea of God excludes any notion of corporeality and lacks, therefore, sensible or imaginary qualities. The idea of an infinite and supremely perfect being by definition lacks any of the limitations associated with what is sensible, as well as any other kind and degree of limitation. For this same reason, the thinking self cannot cause the idea of God. Although the thinking self is not the body, the knowledge that the thinking self possesses about itself includes inherently the awareness of limitations. The very activity of thinking, which is the essence of the thinking self, is evidence of lacks and limitations. Doubting implies lack of certitude, willing implies lack of the end, investigating implies lack of evidence, etc. In other words, the thinking self is inherently deficient and limited. Yet the thinking self possesses an idea, the idea of God, which by definition excludes all limitations. The cause of this idea must have at least as much reality as the idea. In other words, ultimately the cause of this idea must be God himself, even if the thinking self received this idea through some intermediary cause (or causes) that has this idea but is not infinitely perfect being. For, again, the effect cannot exceed the cause.

The thinking self's knowledge of God also must be prior to the thinking self's knowledge of itself. For the standard of judgment is always prior to and the ground for any particular judgment that is based on this standard.[14] From the very beginning of Descartes' investigation, the thinking self has engaged in the making of judgments, claiming that something is uncertain or certain, that something is better or worse, etc. These judgments presuppose the ability to make them, and this ability lies in recognizing what is conditioned in light of what is absolute. I can say that one thing is brighter than another thing because I have some sense of what complete brightness may be, even though I have never experienced an absolute flood of light. Without any knowledge of brightness as such, I could not distinguish and judge degrees and kinds of brightness. This means that, from the very beginning, the thinking self possessed the criterion or standard by which to distinguish degrees and kinds of certainty, degrees and kinds of perfection, etc. It was this criterion or standard that permitted the thinking self to recognize the certainty of its own existence as well as the uncertainty of the senses.

Consequently, God was always present to the thinking self, even prior to its explicit recognition of the certainty of its own existence.[15] From the very beginning, the thinking self has relied on its knowledge of God, since God is absolute perfection—the ultimate standard of every perfection. Consequently, the idea of God must be not only innate to the thinking self but also, in a sense, the most clear and distinct of all the ideas of the

---

14. See Meditation Three, sections 45–46. This is one of the basic insights of Plato's philosophy, as explained above in section I.2a. Of course, Descartes is developing this idea in a very different context.

15. It is central for Descartes to show that the mind indeed possesses the idea of God, that "infinitely perfect being" stands for something positive in the mind, and is not simply a phrase without content. Without demonstrating the real presence of this idea, his argument cannot proceed. He anticipates the objection that "infinite" is not a real idea, but rather only the negation of the finite. In this sense, we only would have a concept of finite things and "infinite" would be simply the negation of these things, but without real content. Similarly, one could say, the term "non-shoe" is not a real concept, but is rather simply a word that negates that about which we do have a concept, namely, "shoe." Descartes faces this objection by claiming that the mind recognizes more reality in an infinite substance than in a finite one, precisely because infinite is the standard by which to judge finite things (see ibid.). Empiricist thinkers, on the other hand, for whom all ideas derive from the senses, will deny that the mind has access to any positive idea of God. See the discussion below on Hobbes (section III.2a), who holds this view.

thinking self. For the knowledge and certainty of God is the source of every other knowledge and certainty, including: I think, therefore I am.[16]

The priority of the idea of God does not imply the absolute knowledge of God. The idea of God is not clear and distinct in this sense. On the contrary, supreme perfection is understood by definition as exceeding the thinking self, which is limited and imperfect in many ways, so that the thinking self cannot understand God in his fullness. However, the priority of the idea of God does imply that the thinking self relies, and has always relied, on God.[17] Just as we judge bright things in virtue of having some prior understanding of pure light, even if we have not experienced a total flood of light, we know all perfections in virtue of having some prior understanding of God, who is supreme perfection. Moreover, just as we see things only in and through the presence of light, we know things (including what is certain about ourselves) only in and through the presence of God, even though we do not know God himself completely.

Since God is absolute perfection, Descartes argues that God cannot be a deceiver, for all deceit is based on some lack, and God lacks nothing.[18] All deceit is a means to accomplish some goal, but God already is the ultimate fulfillment of every goal. Rather, God himself is pure reality—pure truth, which does not admit of any falsehood. As absolute perfection, God is supremely certain, and the source of everything that is certain, of everything that is clear and distinct. Consequently, the truth of every science depends on God, and we can be certain of everything that is clear and distinct because we are certain that God exists and that he is not a deceiver. For, again, God is the basic condition for all certainty, including the first certainty encountered by the thinking self, namely, its own existence.

It is only at this point that Descartes feels confident in using clarity and distinctness as a general scientific principle. For God is the source of the thinking self's own criterion for certainty, as well as the source of the very being of the thinking self. Not only is the certainty that I am in virtue of God, but the reality that I am is also in virtue of God, for being is a perfection and God is the cause of every perfection.[19]

---

16. This might be at least part of Descartes' response to the questions about his procedure, posited in the first paragraph of section III.1c above.

17. Again, this view has a long history, and already is well developed in Augustine. Descartes is developing it in a different framework.

18. See Meditation Three, section 52.

19. Ibid., sections 49–50.

III.1e
The Application of Clear and Distinct Ideas

Now that Descartes has justified the adequacy of clear and distinct ideas as the criterion for certainty, on the grounds that a good God sustains the mind's being and intellectual vision, he is ready to turn his attention to truths pertaining to the external world. As mentioned, his philosophy proceeds from the thinking soul, to God, to the world. The contemplation of God, which to previous philosophers is the highest attainable stage of human wisdom, is in Descartes primarily an argument necessary to certify the adequacy of the mind's clear and distinct ideas, a preliminary step for the investigation of external reality.[20]

Now, concerning the external world, what exactly is clear and distinct? About the thinking self, its existence and activities were evident, such as willing, doubting, etc. About God, his presence to the mind was evident, as well as his existence and the attributes that belong to supremely perfect being. On the other hand, bodies are fundamentally alien to the thinking self, which at first does not even recognize with certitude its relation with its own body.

Accordingly, bodies are clear and distinct to the extent that they can be fixed objects of thought, to the extent that they lend themselves to the analysis of the mind, especially mathematical analysis. The sensible qualities of bodies are not clear and distinct, since they constantly change and produce a variety of appearances. At first, not even the existence of sensible objects was evident to Descartes. However, once he has proved that God is not a deceiver, he reasons that sense stimuli must proceed from real extramental objects, and not from some hidden faculty of the self. If this information would proceed from the self, he would have been aware of it. Otherwise, deceit would be part of his constitution as a thinking thing that is caused by God, which is not possible, since God is not a deceiver.[21]

Hence, the external world of bodies exists, including his own body, by which he relates to other bodies through sensing and imagining, which are properties of a corporeal being. These faculties, unlike pure thinking, always include the concept of extension. On the other hand, the clear and distinct idea of his own existence as a thinking thing does not include the notion of extension. His own essence as a thinking thing is distinct from

---

20. Accordingly, the investigation of bodies is left for last, in Meditation Six.

21. See Meditation Six, sections 79–80.

sensing and imagining, since thinking may be understood without sensing and imagining, while sensing and imagining always presuppose the thinking that is cognizant of them. Hence, these faculties depend on a nature that is different from the thinking self (the pure I), namely, a body or God. Since God is not a deceiver, they must depend on the human body, which is what seems most obvious and evident. If they would come from God, we would be wrong about what appears so evident, and it would be hard to maintain that God is not a deceiver.

All the same, the senses are not to be trusted as sources of certainty.[22] Rather, what is certain about bodies are those features that can be analyzed mathematically. For example, about a piece of wax, the smell, color, and other sensible qualities change. Hence, these qualities are not essential. Rather, the matter or substance of the wax, which underlies the sensible changes, remains. The material substratum, and not its sensible features, is evident to the mind. Hence, this material substratum is clear and distinct to the extent that it can be analyzed according to its inherent properties. These properties are those that lend themselves to mathematical analysis, such as volume, weight, etc., properties that are coextensive with the reality of the body as a body—an extended thing.

Bodies are clear and distinct to the extent that they can be analyzed mathematically.[23] Hence, mathematical sciences that include empirical elements, such as astronomy, can never be as clear and distinct as the pure mathematical sciences, such as arithmetic and algebra.[24] At the same time, the mathematical analysis of bodies discloses fundamental aspects of their behavior, so that they become more predictable and, consequently, usable in terms of technology. In extending the mathematical treatment of nature, Descartes falls in line with the scientific revolution of the sixteenth and seventeenth centuries.

Descartes' quantitative approach to bodies favors mechanistic explanations and dismisses the central feature of classical physics, namely, the final cause.[25] For Aristotle (and for the classical and medieval tradition in general), as noted in chapter 1, the fundamental cause of any thing, whether it be natural or artificial, is its purpose. For natural things, the purpose is

22. Descartes always reminds us that, even concerning doubtful matters, error can be avoided by withholding assent. See Meditation Five, section 62.

23. See Meditation Six, section 80.

24. See Meditation One, section 20.

25. See Meditation Four, section 55.

the form since natural things seek actualization according to their specific form, while the form is the immanent principle governing the growth and development of the thing. For Descartes, this approach, however consonant with everyday experience and speech, has no place in a philosophy of certainty. For the approach is based on common sense observation, insofar as the final cause, as an immanent principle, is inferred from the observed activity of the thing. Moreover, the analysis of substances in terms of form, as a qualitative rather than quantitative analysis, is based on the senses through and through. Rather, properly scientific analysis focuses on what belongs to the constitution and arrangement of bodies as such, namely, on what is clear and distinct about them, rather than on some presumed purpose organizing the body. The focus is on how bodies are constituted, rather than on why. In traditional terms, only the material and the efficient cause remain proper subjects of scientific investigation, the former insofar as it relates to the intrinsic constitution of bodies and the latter insofar as it relates to the interaction among bodies. Again, this general attitude is found in other chief thinkers of this period, such as Francis Bacon (1561–1626).[26]

The dismissal of the final and formal causes was also the dismissal of the understanding of the good in terms of unity. According to the classical understanding, the purpose of each thing is to reach its best state, which is the proper unity according to its specific form. For Aristotle, the human good is (moral and intellectual) virtue. This is the proper unity of the soul, the correct order and functioning of the appetitive, emotive, and intellectual parts of the soul. This unity disposes the human being to perform its proper function well (which is happiness), and performing the function well implies this unity. In other words, working towards the final cause engages and integrates the basic dimensions of the being as a whole, since the good of every being lies in the proper unity according to form. Since the form organizes the being as a whole, excellence—the best condition for a thing—lies in being organized, unified, in the best way. Not surprisingly, philosophy, understood as an activity conducive to the human goal, was

---

26. "Causarum finalium inquisitio sterilis est, et, tanquam virgo Deo consecrata, nihil parit" (Inquiry into final causes is sterile, and, like a virgin consecrated to God, bears nothing). Bacon, *De Dignitate et Augmentis Scientiarum*, III, V, 198. In other words, the study of final causes has no practical applications. Bacon, like Descartes, Hobbes, and others from this period, also stressed the practical aim of science in terms of prediction and control of nature—the increase of human power and comfort through technology. See Descartes' remark in note 30 below. This aspect of Hobbes' thought is discussed in sections 2b–c of this chapter.

seen as rooted in a fundamental and comprehensive desire, not merely in the desire of thinking as divorced from the rest of the self.

On the other hand, Descartes' perspective, rooted in clear and distinct ideas, yields a very different view of the beings of nature. Accordingly, he does not see human reality in terms of one formal and unifying principle governing material and spiritual dimensions, but rather as the coexistence of two distinct things—the thinking thing and the extended thing (body), which are nevertheless closely related.[27] About the human body, and other bodies of nature, what is important is not the ultimate purpose of their structures and activities, but rather their arrangement and constitution in terms of quantifiable or mathematical properties. The third reality in Descartes' philosophy, namely, the divine thing (God), is not considered as a final cause that gives meaning and purpose to the activities of creatures, but rather only as an efficient and preserving cause of creatures. God is the source of certainty for the human mind, but not (at least in terms of purely certain philosophy) the source of meaning, since final causes fall outside the scope of clear and distinct ideas.[28]

III.1f
The Outcome of Descartes' Philosophical Desire

The outcome of this philosophy is proportionate to the desire that grounds it. This desire seeks absolute certainty, and Descartes finds what he is looking for in the self-evidence of thought itself. His desire for certainty finds refuge in the unassailable fortress of pure thought, insofar as thinking can derive certainty from and by itself. To be sure, insofar as the basis of Descartes' philosophy is bound with the recognition of doubt and with the concomitant urge for certitude, his philosophical desire is more than the exigency of pure thought, but has other existential roots. However, the actual evolution of this philosophical desire, as it seeks fulfillment in certitude, does consciously unfold in the exclusive domain of the thinking self, rejecting communication with other parts of the human self. This

27. The central concept in Descartes' metaphysics is "thing" (in Latin, *res*): reality consists of three distinct things—the thinking thing, the divine thing (God), and the extended thing.

28. Descartes recognizes that God may have a variety of purposes, but he considers it futile to inquire into them, since they fall outside the scope of science and philosophy. See Meditation Four, section 55.

separation of thought in its own self-sufficient domain was necessary for the sake of certainty in the sense of absolute self-evidence, for the sake of complete cognitive security.

However, this mode of certainty comes at a high price, insofar as philosophy has cut its ties with other dimensions of existence. Philosophy has become specialized. No longer is philosophy an activity rooted in the whole human being; philosophy is now the activity by which the thinking thing finds certitude. There are, to be sure, historical reasons for this emphasis on certainty, especially in terms of its mistrust of the senses and tradition. After all, this was the time just after one of the most basic and authoritative assumptions, justified by both common sense experience and tradition, and pertaining to the very place of human beings in the universe, had been proven false along with its concomitant cosmology: the view that the earth was stationary and at the center of our universe.

Against this background, however, Descartes' own philosophical project and method are quite original, since what he wants is to establish the very adequacy of the mind's clear and distinct ideas in order to justify their general application. In other words, with Descartes, philosophy has become philosophy of science, the investigation of the roots and properties of scientific knowledge as such. Consequently, it is at this point that philosophy becomes clearly distinct from science; philosophy investigates knowledge itself,[29] while the sciences investigate the different areas of knowledge. Not surprisingly, after Descartes knowledge becomes the central philosophical problem. Even in ethics, the chief question in modern authors like Kant is no longer happiness or the good life, but rather, how can I be sure that I am doing the right thing?

At its core, Cartesian desire is both negative and positive. In a negative sense, the desire seeks removal of doubt, and this removal entails thought's divorce from everything that is doubtful, from everything that is not clear and distinct. The other face of this desire is positive, in two senses. First, thought seeks the establishment of certainty, of cognitive security. Second, thought desires to impose itself on the alien external world, by grabbing hold of what is clear and distinct about it, by mathematizing it, by predicting and controlling it. That the ultimate why of things falls outside

29. In Descartes, this endeavor is still fundamentally metaphysical. What is known clearly and distinctly are things: the thinking thing, the divine thing, and the extended thing. The full title of his main work is *Meditations on First Philosophy*, which recalls the classical understanding of metaphysics as the inquiry into first causes. As shown, however, Descartes' approach is a real break with tradition.

the domain of certitude is irrelevant, since what is desired is mastery, not insight.[30] After all, the external world of nature, including the body, is conceived as fundamentally alien to the thinking self; from this standpoint, the goal cannot be communion with it.

Descartes' investigation of God is also oriented towards justifying the adequacy of scientific knowledge. In terms of his procedure, the discussion of God is not the culmination of the human search for wisdom, whereby all reality is contemplated in the light of its first and divine principle. Indeed God is recognized as superior, transcendent, and as the ultimate cause of reality. However, this recognition does not translate into a desire to gain some insight into the meaning and vestiges of this transcendence, through the analogies and other indirect means available to human beings, let alone through the synthesis of reason and revelation. For this recognition serves a philosophy focused on the certain application of knowledge, rather than one whose fundamental intent is to approach the divine. Accordingly, it is not surprising that with Descartes philosophy finally breaks its ties completely with theology as the science of revelation. Revealed divine wisdom can offer no help to a philosophy centered on the unassailable self-evidence of thought.

The final goal of Cartesian philosophy is the effectiveness of clear and distinct ideas in the external world, rather than the elevation of the soul or the contemplation of God. That his philosophy has this as its first aim does not mean that his philosophy is not theological, although it is not theological in the ancient or medieval sense. His philosophy is not, ultimately, God-oriented. Interestingly, it is, rather, God-based, since God ratifies the adequacy of thought. What ancients and medievals saw as the highest expression of love of wisdom, namely, the consideration of God, in Descartes is but a preliminary step. This difference illustrates the fundamental break represented by Descartes' philosophical conception: the ultimate fruition of philosophy is not elevating both intellect and character towards an ultimate goal, but rather grounding the adequacy of the thinking self's perspective in the face of the external world. Philosophy is now an anchoring activity, securing the legitimacy and effectiveness of knowledge about the world. In a word, love of wisdom becomes something else in Descartes, namely, love of certainty.

30. "It is possible to arrive at knowledge that would be very useful in life and that, in place of that speculative philosophy taught in the schools, it is possible to find a practical philosophy, by means of which . . . we might be able . . . [to] render ourselves, as it were, masters and possessors of nature" (*Discourse on Method*, Part Four, sections 61–62).

III.2
HOBBES AND THE DESIRE FOR SECURITY

Around the same time of Descartes, in England, Thomas Hobbes (1588–1679) developed a very different philosophical conception, which nevertheless shared some of Descartes' basic assumptions. Although Hobbes' philosophy differs vastly from that of Descartes, in terms of positions and interests, both thinkers work within a common modern framework. Within this framework, Hobbes' philosophy represents the other side of the coin, so to speak, with regard to the issue of philosophical desire.

III.2a
Hobbes vs. Descartes on Certainty

At first glance, Hobbes does not seem to be one of those major modern philosophers (such as Hume, Locke, Kant, and Hegel) who follow Descartes in giving the problem of knowledge the central place. After all, most of his writings are devoted to political matters. However, Hobbes bases his political thought on a distinctive conception of human nature, and central to this conception is his account of knowledge.

Like Descartes, Hobbes sees no significant affinity between the human subject and the external, sensible world. The senses do not give us access to objective truth. In Descartes, this basic assumption led to his fundamental developments, such as his seeking refuge in the unassailable realm of thought's clear and distinct ideas. On the other hand, ancient and medieval thinkers assume a basic affinity between the soul (microcosm) and the universe (macrocosm). This is not to say that they take sense experience simply at face value, but rather that to them, even though what is sensible and what is intelligible belong to very different orders, there is a fundamental link between these two orders. This is clear in Aristotle, for whom universal knowledge is abstracted from sensible particulars. This true also for Plato, who, as is well known, does not trust the senses. For Plato, sensible things do remind us of the eternal forms, because they are copies of the forms. There is continuity between the sensible and the intelligible realms, since the former *reflects* the latter. For Descartes, on the other hand, sensible objects have a place in (certain) philosophy not insofar as they are sensible, but only insofar as they are bodies that can be perceived clearly and distinctly, that is, mathematically calculated, predicted, and controlled.

For Hobbes, sense data is a seeming or *fancy*.[31] However, unlike Descartes, Hobbes does not believe that absolute truths lie in a separate realm of pure, self-sufficient thought. To Hobbes, human beings have no access to absolute truth, since human beings are fundamentally physical entities that are always conditioned by time, place, and their interaction with other bodies. The mathematical sciences, such as geometry, are exceptional, since they do provide universal certainty. However, this certainty exists only in the mind, insofar as all minds can agree on the definitions and principles. Truth and certainty are based on agreement, rather than on the mind's access to some fundamental reality that grounds all certainty (for Descartes this reality is God).

Once the link between the intelligible and the sensible orders is broken, according to the modern assumption, at least two philosophical avenues emerge. One avenue is to seek certainty in the realm of pure thought (ideas), in order to impose later this certainty on the external world insofar as this world lends itself to this imposition. This is the avenue of Descartes and of all so-called modern rationalism. The other avenue is to take the sensible world as the only source of what is intelligible, namely, reducing the intelligible to the sensible. After all, at face value, the reality of sense experience seems more evident than the reality of a separate and self-sufficient realm of pure ideas. Perhaps all ideas are merely by-products of sense experience. This is the avenue of Hobbes, and generally that of other modern empiricists, such as John Locke and David Hume.[32] In other words, the same assumption—namely, the radical break between the sensible and the intelligible orders—yields opposite perspectives on knowledge, which are nevertheless two sides of the same coin. This opposition of perspectives about knowledge implies contrasting perspectives on philosophical desire.

For Hobbes, all ideas and knowledge derive ultimately from the senses.[33] This is true even about the idea of God. One may say that God is perfect, omnipotent, infinite, etc. However, when we apply these attributes to God, we do not know what we mean. These attributes are simply names, and all names originally apply to the things we experience. For example, the name *perfect* originally refers to those things of our experience that we consider excellent or complete. When we call God "perfect," however, we

---

31. See *Leviathan*, Part 1, chapter 1, section 4.

32. Still within the modern framework, Kant tries to synthesize these two avenues, as explained below.

33. See *Leviathan*, Part 1, chapter 1, section 2.

have no idea about how God actually is perfect, since (according to faith) God is unlike anything we experience. Similarly, since we experience things that we consider powerful, as well as things that have limitations, we can say that God is all-powerful (omnipotent) or infinite (without limitations), but we really do not know what we mean when we call God these names.[34] Descartes is wrong: we have no idea of God. All our ideas derive, ultimately, from sense experience and God is not a sense object. When we talk about God, we transfer names, which originally refer to the things we sense, to a reality we may believe in but do not know. This rests on our belief, not on any knowledge or idea of God.

III.2b
Hobbes' Account of Knowledge

All ideas come from sense experience, and sense experience is fundamentally the result of the interaction between two bodies. Sensible objects act upon the sense organs (through the intermediation of the nerves) in a physical way, through some motion. For example, noise strikes the ear, a surface makes contact with touch, light and color affect the eye, etc. These actions, by which sensible objects move the sense organs, result in counteractions, namely, in the reactions of the sense organs. These reactions, by which the sense organs bounce back, so to speak, after being pushed by sensible objects, constitute sense experience. Sense experience is simply the various motions undergone by the body through its interaction with other bodies. Sense experience is fancy, insofar as the perceiver believes that what is experienced is truly present in external objects—that the color exists in the surface, that the smell exists in the substance, etc. However, sensible objects cause these experiences *in* the perceiver—or, better, these experiences, which are the by-product of the physical interaction between sensible objects and the human subject, happen in the perceiver. For different bodily subjects react differently, and therefore experience differently, the same sensible object. Sense experience may be similar among perceivers, but strictly speaking, it is unique to the perceiver.[35]

---

34. Ibid., Part 1, chapter 3, section 12.

35. See ibid., Part 1, chapter 1, section 4. Aristotle also maintains that knowledge comes from the senses, yet his account of knowledge is fundamentally different, as explained in section I.3d.

Sensible objects do possess the physical attributes necessary to move the perceiving subject, and the perceiving subject does possess the physical attributes to react to these motions. However, sense experience has more to do with the subject than the object, insofar as sense experience takes place in the subject, since this experience is properly the undergone physical reaction of the subject. Accordingly, sensible qualities, such as color, smell, sound, etc., do not exist in external objects but only in the perceiver. Sensible qualities are *secondary* qualities, since they are not inherent to objects; they are separable by-products existing in the perceiver. The only inherent qualities of sensible objects, the so-called primary qualities, are those inseparable features of bodies as bodies, namely, mass, volume, figure, etc.[36] Accordingly (as Descartes would also say), only the mathematical or quantitative analysis of bodies yields (some) objective or inherent truth about bodies as such.

The things, which were at first vividly and immediately sensed, remain in the memory (also called imagination), which is really a decaying sense—the faculty that retains what was previously sensed, but in a fading form. Although other animals also sense and remember, human beings distinguish themselves through the use of language, since they name those things they have experienced, and communicate and learn from them. Some names are proper, like the name of an individual person, while most names are collective, since they do not refer to a single individual but rather to a group of individuals. All names, however, refer to individuals. Collective names, such as horse (which applies to all horses) or red (which applies to all red things), still apply to individuals, namely, to the sum of individuals that in our experience appear similar in some respect. These names apply to nothing universal. "Horse" does not apply in any sense to the horseness of horses, and "red" does not apply to the redness of red things. They simply apply to those individuals that in our sense experience and memory have appeared similar in certain respects, so that we call them by the same name. As noted, however, each sense experience, and consequently each memory, is unique, strictly speaking.

Through names, the mind organizes its memories and experiences, by calling things that appear similar in some respect(s) by the same name. According to Hobbes, thinking or conceptualizing (as opposed to merely imagining) is really naming, while reasoning is establishing connections

---

36. This distinction between primary and secondary qualities, well developed by John Locke, is fundamental in all modern philosophy.

among names. The faculty of reason, he famously claims, is nothing but a calculator that adds and subtracts, since it establishes relations among names, and names refer to quantities (groups/sums) of individuals.[37] This is the consequence of Hobbes' thoroughly materialistic account of knowledge.

However, naming can be adequate or inadequate, precise or imprecise.[38] Naming is adequate and precise when it refers to those individuals that are meant, and only to those individuals. It is inadequate and imprecise when it is unclear (it fails to capture specifically those individuals that are meant), deceitful (it intentionally misleads), or false (it does not correspond to the individuals that are meant). Hence, the apt use of names, based on careful observation, is the basis of learning and science. Learning is establishing the correspondence between names and what is observed, as well as the right connections among names, which indicate connections among facts (individuals). On the other hand, the inept use of names perpetuates ignorance and error. The inept use of names, even at a basic level, is injurious, not only because it constitutes basic error but also because it stifles progress, since one cannot build upon an erroneous foundation.

Ultimately, the basis for knowledge (accurate naming) is careful observation. The opinions and expressions found in books, even in the most revered and authoritative ones, serve to misguide rather than to instruct, if they are not corroborated by observation. Otherwise, words are accepted without seeing if they correspond to things. Hence, unsophisticated individuals who follow their own natural judgment are better served than those who rely on book learning only. Like Descartes, Hobbes mistrusts received opinion and tradition, but for different reasons. For Descartes, opinions and tradition are received through the senses, and the senses are doubtful; certainty is found in clear and distinct ideas. For Hobbes, on the other hand, all knowledge originates in sense. Opinions and traditions, when taken as authoritative on their own account, may interfere with sounder ways to interpret facts.[39]

For Hobbes, knowledge of the world is always partial at best. This is not surprising considering that he thinks all knowledge originates in sense and that sense is fancy. There is really no affinity between the perceiving subject and the perceived objects, except insofar as both are bodies, and there is no recourse to a separate realm of clear and distinct ideas.

37. See *Leviathan*, Part 1, chapter 5, sections 1–2.
38. See ibid., Part 1, chapter 4, sections 3–4.
39. See ibid., Part 1, chapter 4, section 13.

Moreover, even though certain patterns may be observed among the instances of sense experience, in the behavior of bodies, future exceptions are always possible. Knowledge is always an approximation. We measure and calculate the behavior of bodies, so that we can more or less predict their behavior in the future. With Hobbes, as with Descartes, we see the emphasis on mathematical analysis as a tool to grab hold of the external world, understood as the realm of bodies.

This analysis, however, helps us understand how bodies behave, but not why. For Hobbes, the mind sees only the surface, so to speak, of the material world (and perhaps the surface is all there is), insofar as all ideas are the by-products of the physical interaction between the human body and other bodies. This interaction does not disclose the natures, essences, or purposes of bodies (whatever these words may mean), but rather only their material effects on each other and on the human body. With Hobbes, as with Descartes, formal and final causes fall outside the realm of science, which focuses only on the interaction (efficient causality) and constitution (material cause) of bodies. Human knowledge can establish the conditions for certain effects, but not their natures and purposes. Science is knowledge of the consequences among names and, thereby, facts, and its aim is prediction and control—mastery over nature.[40] Its benefits are practical—increase in comforts and technological advancement. This view of the purpose of science, though part of a different philosophy, is also reminiscent of Descartes.

Faith and religion do speak about the ultimate purpose of things, but this falls outside the realm of science. With Hobbes, as with Descartes, philosophy has become totally separate from faith, not because of a change in theological beliefs but because of a change in philosophy itself, whose fundamental concern has become investigating how and to what extent the mind can know and control the external world. Accordingly, Hobbes begins his major political work, *Leviathan*, with the discussion of knowledge, in order to lay the foundation for his understanding of political reality.

III.2c
The Purpose and Value of Knowledge in Hobbes

For Hobbes, reason, knowledge, and science (the most developed form of knowledge) are ancillary resources that serve practical ends. They serve what Hobbes calls the passions, such as material ambition, desire for power,

40. See ibid., Part 1, chapter 5, sections 17 and 21.

and above all fear.[41] Hobbes' position that reason is a calculator in the service of the passions is not surprising, considering his thoroughly materialist understanding of human nature. Human beings are bodies that naturally collide with and seek to overcome other bodies (even sense experience is a form of collision among perceiver and perceived). Above all, they seek self-preservation, but they are also governed by physical urges and forces that often endanger the well-being of other bodies. The purpose of knowledge is accomplishing the ends of material (human) nature.

In this vein, freedom is understood as the unhindered pursuit of material wants, whether it be power (control of bodies), satisfaction of appetites, or security (self-preservation). There is no sense of freedom as rising above the necessities, demands, and interests of physical existence. The classical sense of freedom as the pursuit of wisdom for its own sake, or even freedom as the autonomy of thought as understood by some moderns, is absent. Reason is merely instrumental. Likewise, the will is not in any sense an independent faculty, but rather simply an equivocal name, referring to the given particular desire preceding a course of action.[42] In brief, the springs of human action are physical tendencies and impulses, whose purpose is their own advancement and satisfaction. Strictly speaking, these motives vary according to the variety of human bodies and the circumstances surrounding them.

However, these bodily passions express themselves according to the way the world appears to the subject, within the bounds of human cognition. Especially important in this regard is the sense of isolation in human experience, a by-product of the individualistic nature of cognition: ultimately, individuals have a unique perspective of the world, based on their own physical circumstances. Human bodies are not naturally equipped to trust each other, especially when they compete for the same things. Rather, their mutual diffidence inclines them to attack and eliminate one another, since each sees the other as potentially dangerous or detrimental to their success. Accordingly, war is the product of fear. Attack is the natural form of defense (and therefore justified), the way to eliminate the competition and source of fear. Human beings encroach upon each other, insofar as their

---

41. "According to Hobbes, his mother went into labor when she heard that the Spanish Armada was approaching, so that, as he put it, 'fear and I were born twins together.' This familiar tale indicates how Hobbes himself appreciated the central conjunction of mortal fear and human nature in his own thinking and in his life as well" (Morgan, *Classics of Moral and Political Theory*, 575). Hobbes recognizes the central role of fear, and the concomitant desire for security, in his own philosophy.

42. See *Leviathan*, Part 1, chapter 6, section 53.

tendency is self-preservation and material advancement. Hobbes therefore conceives human beings in their natural state as isolated individuals in complete freedom and, consequently, in mutual conflict—the war of every man against every man. In this chaotic state, human beings have absolute freedom, but no security; fear is continual. The state of nature is therefore, ironically, one from which human beings naturally seek to escape. Through rational calculation, they can form a contract designed to guarantee basic rights (such as self-preservation) by limiting natural, unhindered freedom (such as the freedom to destroy one another).[43] This is now society, an artificial rather than a natural state.[44]

Accordingly, moral virtue, unlike the senses and the passions, is in no sense inherent to human nature, since it does not apply to human beings in isolation. Since it only has meaning in society, moral virtue is an artificial rather than a natural quality. Morality becomes equivalent to law; there is no right and wrong until there is a law to approve and prohibit certain actions. And law is understood strictly in terms of limiting natural rights for the sake of order and security. Morals have no meaning in the natural state, the war of every man against every man. On the contrary, force and fraud are the "virtues" in the state of nature, since they are the best means for self-preservation and success in this war.[45] Lost is the classical sense of virtue as immanent, as the health of the soul, as something worthy for its own sake.

III.2d
Hobbes' Philosophical Desire with Reference to That of Descartes

Within a common modern framework, Descartes and Hobbes offer two contrasting views and, thereby, two faces of philosophical desire. As noted,

43. See ibid., Part 1, chapters 13–14.

44. The state thus created needs sufficient power to "keep them all in awe" (ibid., 13, section 8), so that the fear of punishment outweighs the inclination to violate the agreed-upon rights of others. Fear is not eliminated within the state, but rather redirected towards one authority. The universal fear in the war of every man against every man becomes fear of the sovereign, which ensures order and security to the extent that each citizen can rely on others obeying the law precisely because of this common fear. For Hobbes, this principle also applies to other political states that do not originate in contract, but in force: they can keep order when fear of the ruling power outweighs the desire to subvert.

45. See ibid., Part 1, chapter 13, section 13.

if love of wisdom means anything in Descartes, it means love of certainty. On the other hand, if love of wisdom means anything in Hobbes, it means desire for security. A central element of the desire grounding the philosophies of Descartes and Hobbes is capturing what is seen as an alien, external world. If there is a common core to modern philosophical desire, it is this desire to determine that realm with which the human subject no longer recognizes a basic affinity, what is still often spoken of as the outside world. Naturally, Hobbes articulates this attitude in terms consistent with his own perspective.

According to Hobbes, even though there have always been and will always be individuals unwilling to give up any liberties through political association—individuals committed to the satisfaction of their passions without any regard for their own security or that of others—these individuals are the extreme few. For Hobbes, reason naturally leads to the formation of political states, since peace and security (albeit at the expense of some liberties) are preferable to chaos and its universal fear (albeit in complete liberty). Although human desires vary according to the variety of human bodies, all bodies desire the security to pursue their own satisfaction. Philosophy can be placed within this general concern for security, insofar as philosophy, especially political philosophy, considers the principles and conditions for the security and advancement of human agents. In other words, philosophy is the broadest cognitive expression of the basic human interest in security. As such, philosophy is fundamentally practical in Hobbes' terms, driven by material well-being.

The desire for knowledge is the desire to *know how* to live well in material terms. This may be the specific knowledge of what is beneficial for a particular body, or the broader knowledge of what is generally beneficial for all bodies. In this latter sense, philosophical desire generates political philosophy, as exemplified by Hobbes' *Leviathan*.

∞

For Hobbes, happiness consists in the fulfillment of the passions rather than in the fulfillment of the whole self as governed by reason. For reason is understood as a calculator in the service of the passions. The pursuit of knowledge is valuable only insofar as knowledge is more practically effective than ignorance.[46] In this regard, (political) philosophy can have universal value, since it investigates the principles of political order and security.

46. Hobbes' distinction between the terms *prudence* and *sapience* (two kinds of

However, within the political order, happiness is now understood as an individual or private affair, consisting in the fulfillment of those passions that matter to a given human body. Choosing philosophy as a means to happiness is also an individual affair. The philosophical life, whatever one might mean by this, will be one among many equally legitimate ways to seek individual satisfaction. For Hobbes, philosophy is a specialized activity, as it was for Descartes, but for different reasons. For Descartes, philosophy is specialized and fragmented, since it is rooted in only one dimension of the self—pure thought. For Hobbes, on the other hand, it is rooted in the physical (to which all is reduced), in the passions that rule the calculations of reason. Philosophy, as an activity, is specialized and fragmented, since it is the expression of one among many passions and drives within political reality.

Within the frameworks of Descartes and Hobbes, love of wisdom is no longer seen as the highest expression and fulfillment of human nature considered in its totality, since the very concept of human nature has changed, so that this concept now lacks the unity it possessed in ancient and medieval thought. In these moderns, philosophical desire is expressive of a particular dimension of human reality. Consequently, philosophical interest, as well as philosophical fulfillment, is also particular rather than comprehensive.

Love of wisdom, by losing the unity of its foundation, by becoming rooted in what is particular in human existence, also lost the unity of its vision. For what is sought (and found) is proportionate to the desire that seeks. Also for these reasons, philosophy has become a stranger to humanity, since it no longer understands its task chiefly as the cultivation of what is fundamentally human. Rather, it has become, to this very day, increasingly absorbed into the pursuit of specialized interests, the cultivation of specialized talents, the development of specialized vocabulary, the production of new and specialized scholarship, even among students of ancient and medieval thought.

---

wisdom) makes this attitude clear: "As much experience, is *prudence*; so, is much science *sapience*. For though we usually have name of wisdom for them both, yet the Latins did always distinguish between *prudentia* and *sapientia*; ascribing the former to experience, the latter to science. But to make their difference appear more clearly, let us suppose one man endued with an excellent natural use and dexterity in handling his arms; and another to have added to that dexterity, an acquired science, of where he can offend, or be offended by his adversary, in every possible posture or guard: the ability of the former would be to the ability of the latter, as prudence is to sapience; both useful; but the latter infallible." Ibid., Part 1, chapter 5, section 21.

At this point, however, we shall look at three additional modern philosophers, namely, Kant, Hegel and Nietzsche, which will help us see more fully the transformation of philosophical desire in the modern period.

III.3
KANT: REDEFINING RATIONAL AUTONOMY

Immanuel Kant (1724–1804) continues working within the basic modern framework that is common to Descartes and Hobbes, namely, with the understanding that the fundamental task of philosophy is to establish the extent to which the mind can know the separate, outside world. However, Kant is also a seminal thinker who develops and synthesizes tendencies seen in Descartes and Hobbes. In more than one respect, to understand Kant is also to understand the nature, limits, and possibilities of modern philosophy. As with the other thinkers included in this book, the treatment of Kant is restricted to those elements of his philosophy that bear upon the question of philosophical desire. With Kant, the fragmented and specialized nature of modern philosophical desire becomes even more palpable. This happens as Kant discusses issues such as knowledge, freedom, and God, the very issues through which the more unified vision and desire of the ancients and medievals is manifested. First, however, it is necessary to say a few words on the intellectual background against which Kant formulates his fundamental positions.

III.3a
Kant's Background: Newton and Hume

Like virtually all modern philosophers, Kant is deeply influenced by the new science that develops in the sixteenth and seventeenth centuries and that culminates in the work of Isaac Newton (1643–1727). Central to this new scientific approach is a revised understanding of motion, which rejects the traditional Aristotelian explanation. To Aristotle, the movement of things depends on their specific nature or form, the principle that governs locomotion, growth, alteration, and coming and ceasing to be. For example, a horse runs, grows, and changes in a way that is specific to horses, in a way that is determined by a certain life-principle or form. Aristotle's explanation of motion applies not only to beings on earth (which are subject to generation and corruption) but also to the heavenly bodies. According to common sense experience, the earth seems solid and stationary, while the stars, which appear luminous, light, and everlasting, exhibit uniform motion around the earth. The motion of the stars, according to Aristotle, must be proportionate to their specific constitution according to form and matter. This constitution is fundamentally intellectual, since the heavenly bodies display a higher degree of life than even rational animals (the highest grade of earthly life). For their activity appears uniform and everlasting. Moreover, their matter must be a fifth material principle (quintessence), different from the four earthly elements, since heavenly matter does not alter.

To Aristotle, the heavenly bodies move uniformly and everlastingly because their activity (intellectual contemplation) is their end. Unlike the lower beings of the world of generation and corruption, which exhibit diverse and interrupted motions insofar as they seek various means to reach their ends, the heavenly bodies are already fully accomplished, fully happy, since their purpose is identical to their activity. Accordingly, their locomotion is also perfect, namely, circular, since of all types of locomotion circular motion is the only motion that can remain uniform and perpetual. This is the motion most akin to pure actuality, since the only change or potentiality involved is with respect to place. As such, the heavenly bodies approximate the first principle or unmoved mover, which is pure actuality, more than sublunary beings. In brief, for Aristotle, all motion, earthly and heavenly, is explained through form.[47]

The traditional astronomy of Aristotle and Ptolemy was supplanted as the Copernican heliocentric theory gained support and verification through the work of men like Galileo, Kepler, and, finally, Newton. Central to Newtonian science is a new and universal explanation of motion based, not on form, but on quantitative concepts. The mathematical law of gravity now explains the movement of bodies on earth and in outer space through concepts such as mass, velocity, acceleration, space, and time. Rather than a cosmos governed by natures or forms, each in its proper place, in Newton we have a world consisting of bodies, considered precisely as bodies, interacting within the coordinates of space and time.[48] Through this mathemati-

---

47. The transition from ancient to modern science, and the evolution of the latter culminating in Newton, is developed in Burtt, *The Metaphysical Foundations of Modern Science.*

48. See ibid., chapter 7.

cal or quantitative lens, the beings of nature are now considered *uniformly*, rather than according to specific differences.

With Newton science has become the quantitative assessment of bodies, and causality has become equivalent with the mathematical law, which explains *how* bodies behave in space and time. Not surprisingly, with the advent of the new science, we encounter the first real break between philosophy and science, on the one hand, as well as the total separation between faith and reason that marks the end of medieval philosophy. In the classical world, there was, to be sure, a clear distinction among the different sciences according to their various subject matters. However, the sciences were all part of philosophy, in the sense that the different sciences contributed to a unified vision of reality. Conversely, they contributed to one vision because the sciences were themselves philosophical: their aim was understanding the nature and purpose of the things they studied, so that they could be understood within the general order of the cosmos.

In stark contrast, formal and final causes are excluded from the modern scientific approach, as well as from what philosophy deems objective in the outside world (as already seen in the work of Descartes and Hobbes). Rather, the aim of science is understanding how bodies behave and interact mathematically in space and time, regardless of their specific form. The mathematical law is, in a sense, the new formal cause. Generally expressed as a formula, this law indicates in quantitative terms the mechanisms that govern the behavior of bodies. However, this new formal cause is no longer indicative of any immanent principle governing the very nature and purpose of beings. The classic formal cause, understood in its basic qualitative and purposive sense, is lost together with the final cause, which was understood as the goal of the form.

To be sure, the pioneers of this new science, who were also philosophers, understood its fundamental assumptions, such as the mechanistic view of nature. However, science and philosophy parted ways rather quickly. Science remains focused on external bodies, while philosophy becomes attached to the human knower. Philosophy turns into the investigation of the origin and adequacy of human knowledge, including the possibility of science. This break between science and philosophy is, in a sense, inevitable. The very success at discovery by the new mathematical science, with its revised employment of empirical data, brings up the question, to what extent are human beings equipped to know things outside the mind? Another fundamental question, for Kant especially, is the following:

if necessary (mathematical) laws govern nature, does human freedom exist, and if so, in what sense?

Naturally, these questions fall outside the daily work of modern science, whose aim is discovery in the field of bodies, as well as outside faith, since these questions seek to know what the mind can accomplish on its own account. Yet, these questions are central philosophically within the modern framework. As already discussed, addressing these questions, especially the first, is determinative in Descartes and Hobbes. They also will be for Kant. Concerning the question of knowledge, Kant develops his position primarily in response to the empiricist tradition, particularly David Hume (1711–1776). In turn, Kant's position regarding knowledge serves as the basis for his conception and defense of freedom. For even though nature is mechanistic, reason's access to universal principles assures its autonomy, with regard to both speculative and practical knowledge.

David Hume, however, denies that the mind has any access to universal principles. Hume claims (like Hobbes) that all ideas are reducible to sense impressions. On this thoroughly empirical basis, Hume also argued that since every sense impression is discrete, every idea (as derived from a particular sense impression) is also discrete. Hence, since human beings only sense the succession of things and events, not the causal connections between them, the mind has no idea or knowledge of causality. Accordingly, the mind has no necessary knowledge of the world. By custom, we become acquainted with what generally happens and can, therefore, feel confident that certain things probably will happen in the future, but we can never know this for sure. All we experience with the senses is that certain things accompany others, but not the reasons why they are related. Without access to the causal link, our "knowledge" is only probable, not necessary, since only knowledge of the causal link could assure us that one thing must imply the other. As it stands, all we can say about facts is that a given thing probably relates to another.[49]

On the other hand, it is possible to find necessary relations among ideas, insofar as certain ideas by definition imply others. For example, the idea of an apple by definition implies the idea of fruit, since an apple is by definition a fruit. To say that an apple is not a fruit is a contradiction, since it amounts to saying that an apple is not an apple. As he puts it, "Nothing is demonstrable unless the contrary implies a contradiction."[50] To Hume,

---

49. See Hume, *Enquiry Concerning Human Understanding*, Section 7, Part 2.

50. Hume, *Dialogues Concerning Natural Religion*, 55.

then, the knowledge of necessary connections is, ultimately, tautological, and it is restricted to ideas themselves, not facts. Some sciences, such as logic and mathematics, do yield universal and necessary knowledge, precisely because these sciences consider what is already in the mind, rather than extramental existence.[51]

III.3b
Between Hume and Descartes

Kant only partially accepts the empiricist position of Hume. True, all knowledge begins with experience (i.e., sense). However, against Hume, not all knowledge is reducible to experience. The mind also contributes something to experience, insofar as experience is received according to the mode of the receiver (to use a medieval adage), according to the structures by which the mind assimilates experience. Kant calls what the mind contributes to experience *a priori* knowledge, knowledge that exists in virtue of the mind itself, independently of what it gathers from experience.

A priori knowledge is either knowledge found in concepts or knowledge found in judgments. An example of the former is the concept of substance: even though in our minds we may remove all sensible features from an object, we cannot remove that feature by which the object is thought of as a substance. In other words, the concept of substance does not come from experience; it is something that the mind brings to experience in order to make sense of experience.[52] Other categories, such as time and place, are also a priori modes of understanding, by which the mind organizes experience.[53] Of themselves, however, these a priori concepts or categories are empty. In order for them to have any scientific meaning or objective reference, the supplement of experience is necessary. For they do not refer to any subsistent realities, but rather only to the ways in which the mind assimilates reality, that is, *experienced* reality.

Kant agrees with Descartes' recognition that thought is not reducible to experience, but disagrees with a philosophy that tries to access reality purely through ideas, independently of all experience. For this reason, Descartes' argument for the existence of God, based on the idea of God,

---

51. See *An Enquiry Concerning Human Understanding*, Section 4, Part 1.

52. See Kant, *Critique of Pure Reason*, Introduction to the Second Edition, II, B 6.

53. This is a departure from Newton, who saw space and time as extramental, absolute categories.

is illegitimate for Kant. Although the idea of God may be present to the mind, the mind cannot infer the existence of God purely from this idea, since the knowledge of existence comes from experience (intuition), which is precisely what is lacked concerning God.[54] In this regard, Kant falls in line with Hume.

A priori knowledge is also found in judgments, whose properties are universality and necessity. As Hume rightly pointed out, everything that is experienced through the senses is limited (we cannot experience all possible cases of a given phenomenon) and therefore, strictly on empirical grounds, probable at best. Experience cannot provide universal and necessary knowledge. If such knowledge exists in the mind, this knowledge must be a priori, rather than from experience (a posteriori). True, Hume granted the universality and necessity of certain relations of ideas, insofar as some ideas by definition imply others. In Kant's terms, Hume did grant a priori, analytic judgments, whereby the predicate is included in the subject, as in the proposition "all apples are fruits." Even though the concepts (apple and fruit) in the judgment are derived from experience, the judgment can be considered a priori insofar as we know, in advance of all possible experience, that any apple encountered in the future will be a fruit, since otherwise the object is not an apple in the first place. However, the knowledge provided by the judgment is still definitional or tautological, for it is included in the subject. Accordingly, analytic judgments do not supply any knowledge that is not already included in the concept of the subject.

Only synthetic judgments, judgments in which the predicate is really added to the subject, constitute new knowledge. All a posteriori judgments, which are based on experience, are synthetic, such as the judgment that icy roads are dangerous for driving, and the like. In these judgments, the predicate is not included in the subject, since the predicate is connected to the subject through experience. However, precisely because the judgment is based on experience, it is not universal and necessary; rather, there are possible exceptions.

Is there any evidence of synthetic, a priori judgments? If they do exist, they would show that the mind contributes to experience not only at the level of simple concepts or categories. Their existence would show, in addition, that the mind can have insight into necessary truths (some concerning the very structure of the world of experience) that are not supplied through

---

54. See Kant, *Critique*, "Transcendental Dialectic," B 626; B 630. See also Kant, *Prolegomena*, Conclusion, sections 361–62.

experience alone. According to Kant, these judgments can be shown to exist in the chief branches of science, namely, mathematics, physics, and metaphysics.

In mathematics, even simple calculations, such as "eight plus seven equals fifteen," are a priori, synthetic judgments. The predicate (sum) is not included in the subject (the joining of eight and seven), since the sum is not accessible in the mere juxtaposition of the two numbers to be added, but rather reached through counting (at least the first time we learn why eight and seven equals fifteen). In other words, this judgment is synthetic, since the predicate is really supplied to the subject. At the same time, the truth of the judgment is universal and necessary. That mathematical propositions are not only a priori, but also synthetic, is all the more evident in more complex mathematical operations, where answers must be worked out through various steps.[55]

In physics, the following judgment is synthetic a priori: "In all material changes, the quantity of matter remains equal." For the concept of matter does not include the concept of permanence. Yet, upon reflection, the judgment is universal and necessary. In metaphysics, Kant uses the following example of a synthetic, a priori judgment: "Everything that happens has a cause." For, again, in this case the predicate is not included in the subject. "That which happens" does not include by definition the concept of cause. The predicate is supplied, not from experience, but from the application of a logical principle, namely, that occurrences cannot come from nothing but rather must derive from something.[56]

The chief concern in Kant is establishing the scope of a priori knowledge, the scope of the autonomous dimension of the mind. In a sense, Kant's concern is still Cartesian, even though his method and conclusions are distinct in several ways. What distinguishes Kant's own approach is that unlike Descartes, who proceeds from the mind to extramental reality, and unlike Hobbes (and Hume), who proceeds from sensible things to the mind, Kant combines both approaches. His project aims fundamentally at a clear distinction between that which the mind receives from experience and that which the mind contributes to experience. In this project, tradition and authority are of little or no use (the same status that they hold in Descartes and Hobbes), since all evidence will be gathered through the mind's self-analysis against the background of experience. To proceed

55. *Critique*, Introduction to the Second Edition, V, 1, B 15–16.
56. Ibid., V, 2–3, B 18.

otherwise would be to proceed, in Kant's terms, dogmatically rather than philosophically. In this regard, Kant has adopted the modern framework, whereby philosophical activity springs from a subject that has set itself over and against a separate, outside world.

III.3c
Autonomy and Self-Knowledge

Kant defines his project as *transcendental* philosophy, philosophy based on the mind's self-investigation, focusing on the ways in which the mind thinks and experiences.[57] Kant's fundamental drive is cognitive self-exploration. In this respect, Kant grounds his philosophy on an impulse that is, at face value, classical, reminiscent of that of Socrates, namely, the desire for self-knowledge. However, insofar as Kant is working within the modern framework, insofar as he has defined the environment of his reflection in terms of the mind's distinction from and relation to the objective world outside, the vital source of his philosophy is different from the vital source of classical philosophy. For, again, his transcendental philosophy seeks to distinguish what inherently belongs to the mind from what is received by the mind. The fundamental aim is self-determination, through laying bare the autonomous dimension of the knowing subject, the aspect of cognition that is not reducible to experience.

For this reason, the gold sought through Kant's digging within the self is not the classical one, not the achievement of self-integration in terms of the whole soul, but rather the clear separation of the rational from the empirical (which corresponds to the separation, basic to modern philosophy, between mind and the outside world).[58] The purpose of this separation is the informed application of the former on the latter. In the field of speculative philosophy, the precise assessment of the scope, properties, and limits of pure reason will ensure the proper application of reason as an instrument of knowledge. In the field of practical or moral philosophy, the clear separation of the rational (noumenal) self, as the autonomous source of moral understanding, will provide the moral basis for the rational agent's activity in the empirical world.[59] In other words, the vital source of Kant's philosophy is pure reason's desire for self-determination, on the one hand,

---

57. Ibid., VII.

58. See *Grounding for the Metaphysics of Morals*, Preface, sections 387–89.

59. See ibid., Preface, section 390.

and for imposing itself effectively on the separate empirical world, on the other hand.

Kant's desire for self-knowledge develops according to the preset parameters that ground modern philosophy.[60] Adopting the basic separation between the mind and the outside world, his fundamental aim is distinguishing cognitive autonomy. In turn, this autonomy can only be defined as that which is set over and against the empirical world, as that which can impose itself effectively (speculatively and practically) on the outside world (which includes the empirical self). In other words, Kant's desire for self-knowledge is not the desire to know the human being in its totality, but rather to grab hold of precisely that aspect which can be discerned outside of the totality. In speculative philosophy, the goal is apprehending pure reason in itself, namely, independently of experience. In moral philosophy, the goal is apprehending pure practical reason, as dissociated from emotions, appetites, and other dimensions of concrete existence.

Kantian autonomy is not, like classical autonomy, ordering the totality, but rather escape from the totality, abolishing the very idea of totality. Interestingly, this escape can never be a step towards reunion, towards synthesis with that from which there was escape. In Kant's framework, reunion or synthesis can only mean confusion, precisely because separation is a precondition for clarity. In order for reason to come to light as the instrument for knowledge and as the source of morality, reason must be drawn out of the empirical world. In order to have assurance that reason is indeed serving as the instrument for knowledge and as the source of morality, reason must impose itself on the empirical world, rather than be one in any genuine sense with this world. In other words, Kant's own desire for certainty binds him to a form of dualism that is not merely epistemic, but also ontological. For his concern is not merely envisaging (clearly and distinctly) the autonomy of reason against the empirical world, but also tracing (clearly and distinctly) the interaction of autonomous reason with this world, assuring himself that the interaction never compromises the autonomy. Accordingly, this dualism is constituted by disproportionate sides: that elusive and confined aspect of the mind—pure or a priori cognition—on the one side, and concrete existence, on the other.

60. Kant's approval of Socrates' moral awareness (in ibid., First Section, section 404) is not a return to the ancient approach.

III.3d
The Drive for Moral Self-Determination

Nowhere does this attitude, and its contrast with classical philosophy, surface more clearly than in his ethics, where any commingling of reason with the motives and yearnings of human nature (such as happiness) is seen as possibly contaminating moral worth.[61] For Kant, human beings belong to two separate realms. As rational beings, they belong to the noumenal realm, to the realm of a priori or pure reason. Insofar as they physically live, grow, and experience, insofar as they possess bodies, appetites, feelings, etc., human beings belong to the empirical world. As seekers of happiness, human beings belong to the empirical world, since happiness is the satisfaction of human nature and its inclinations.[62] To Kant, the ethical question is not, as it was for the ancients, what is true happiness, what is the most excellent and fulfilling way of life. To Kant, all versions of happiness are equally defective as principles in a system of morality. For all versions of happiness are grounded in human nature, which belongs to the empirical world.

Rather, the key to morality is for human beings to ground themselves in the realm of autonomous reason. Morality consists in reason's recognition of its inherent universal principles, principles that are not derived from the empirical world but that should be imposed on the empirical world. Kant sees the strength and uniqueness of his conception of morality in the fact that it is not based on human nature and experience at all, but rather only on a priori reason. Freedom and autonomy are based on rational principles, purified from everything empirical. They cannot be found in the empirical world, which is conditioned and mechanistic. Accordingly, the goal is not to unify all dimensions of the soul, as it was for the ancients, but rather to dissociate those pure rational principles of morality from every other dimension of human existence. To Kant, unity of soul can never mean proper order, as it was for the ancients, but only the confusion of rational and empirical principles.

In terms of the moral life, the goal is the imposition of rational principles, which is possible to the degree that empirical principles are excluded. Actions based on experience, the evaluation of consequences, or the inclinations of human nature are actions based on conditioned, rather than free, principles. These actions may bring happiness, and be practical, expedient,

---

61. See ibid., First Section, sections 398–99.

62. See ibid., First Section, sections 399 and 405.

and even beneficial, but they are not moral or free in any genuine sense. Only reason, purified from everything empirical, can be the autonomous source of knowledge and moral action. Morality, like the empirical world, obeys laws. The difference is that the laws of morality are freely determined by reason, while the physical laws of nature are not.[63]

The chief moral principle, and the basis for all other moral precepts, is what Kant calls the categorical imperative. This rational principle dictates what should be done, in a universal sense. It is the most general and fundamental moral law, since its basis is universality itself, namely, reason's recognition of and respect for universality, on the positive side, and reason's inherent rejection of inconsistency and contradictoriness, on the negative side. For reason recognizes that what is morally valid is valid universally for all agents, itself included. To make oneself the exception is to contradict oneself, to violate the exigencies of reason itself. Accordingly, the moral law should be followed regardless of individual circumstances, consequences, or inclinations. The core of all moral obedience and worth is reason's recognition of and respect for its own inherent law(s), the commitment to universal consistency. Hence, the most general expression of the moral law (the categorical imperative) is: "I should never act except in such a way that I can also will that my maxim should become a universal law."[64] This is a law that reason should respect and obey, but it is also free, insofar as reason determines it autonomously, within the scope of reason itself.

Kant insists that morality's force lies in being grounded in pure reason, rather than experience, and that therefore a moral system should not be based on examples from life, practical considerations, or inclinations. However, Kant does offer a few examples. One example of the application of the categorical imperative concerns the question of lying: should I lie if I am in a difficult situation? Kant responds that only telling the truth can become a universal law, and therefore only this course of action can correspond to the categorical imperative. On the other hand, a law that allows lying destroys itself, because it contradicts itself. Lying can exist because it passes for truth. A universal law that allows lying abolishes the possibility for lying, since no one would believe another. Against the objection that this example draws from experience (since we know from experience the conditions for effective lying), Kant would probably say that the force of the

---

63. See ibid., Preface, section 388; First Section, section 402, n. 14.
64. Ibid., First Section, section 402.

example is reason's recognition of the universality of truth, and the recognition that universality admits of no exceptions.

Kant's main objective is to evidence the autonomy of moral reason, rather than to provide a practical code for concrete, day-to-day living. The difficulty, of course, is that morality, to the degree that it involves actions, and not only the recognition of universal rational principles, also involves the intervention of the empirical self in the empirical world. The core of the difficulty is distinguishing the extent to which moral principles, rather than empirical principles, govern actions, in order to determine moral worth. To Kant, an action has moral worth when it is determined solely by duty to the moral law, rather than by empirical motives.[65] The person who follows the moral law for the very sake of the moral law possesses, in Kant's terms, a good will. The good will is the only good without qualification, since a good will is good inherently, in virtue of its very willing, as opposed to other so-called human goods, such as intelligence and strength, which may or may not be good depending on their use.

As noted, every morally pertinent action has some effect in the empirical world and engages the empirical self, the concrete human being with desires, emotions, experiences, relations, community, etc. The agent acts morally when he or she acts in virtue of the moral law, regardless of empirical factors. However, these factors never can be a matter of complete indifference to the empirical self. Following the moral law in concrete actions and situations is, for the empirical self, relatively difficult or easy, pleasant or unpleasant, convenient or inconvenient, advantageous or disadvantageous, etc.

What happens when empirical elements agree with the determination of autonomous reason, in cases where, for example, the empirical self enjoys following the moral law, or has other interests associated with following the moral law, such as increase in prestige or economic advantage? In these cases, determining moral worth is virtually impossible, since it is not clear, even to the agent, whether the action is performed in virtue of the moral law or in virtue of personal inclinations. For in these cases, reason and inclination become fused together in the action, since they both stand behind the one action. It is not clear whether either source would have produced the action independently of the other, so that acting according to the moral law is not definitive evidence for acting *in virtue* of the moral

---

65. See ibid., Second Section, sections 440–41.

law.[66] Naturally, only acting in virtue of the moral law entails moral worth, since, after all, people can align their actions with the dictate of the moral law for a variety of ulterior purposes. The person who understands the demands of reason, and also has personal motives to follow these demands, by definition obscures the issue of moral worth, since it is not clear whether this person would still act according to the moral law if his or her personal motives would conflict with the moral law. In a word, it is not clear whether this person is acting in virtue of the moral law or not.

Even the person who makes some personal sacrifice in following the moral law, but derives some other benefit(s) (even a benefit as intangible as the satisfaction of personal pride), still can obscure the issue of moral worth. For it is possible that this person still would act according to the moral law in virtue of the latter benefit(s) alone. Accordingly, for Kant, the only times when moral worth is clear are cases in which the agent follows the moral law, in spite of all the interests of the empirical self. In other words, moral worth comes to light through the total division and conflict between the moral and the empirical self, in the cases where the moral law is followed even though all personal motives are against it.[67] However, one wonders if finding pure cases like this is even possible, and Kant himself has his doubts on the matter. It could be, upon further analysis, that some hidden empirical motive exists, that could suffice in leading the agent to act according to the moral law, and which therefore questions if the agent acted in virtue of the moral law in the first place.

However this may be, Kant's practical recommendation is not for people to become haters of the moral law with their entire empirical being, yet followers of the moral law in virtue of their a priori reason. Rather, his main concern is establishing the principles of moral autonomy and freedom, which requires their recognition outside the field of nature and experience.

66. In this regard, Kant is emphasizing goodness in terms of efficient, rather than final, causality.

67. Kant does not wish to convey that it is ideal, in terms of daily life, always to have evil inclinations that are nevertheless suppressed by reason (e.g., someone dedicated to saving lives despite his vocation as a serial killer). Rather, he tries to find indicators of the autonomy of reason: only when all empirical motives are excluded is universal reason proven to be the cause of the action. Again, this shows that Kant's primary concern is defining the field of (moral) reason, rather than living and acting well in the concrete. His primary question is, how can I be sure that I am acting morally? In this sense, his concern is still certainty, as with Descartes. The obvious contrast is with Aristotle, who claims that the study of ethics aims at action more than theory (*Nicomachean Ethics* 1.3) and at reaching happiness (ibid., 1.7).

On the other hand, Kant is far from embracing the unity and happiness of the entire self as a principle of ethics. To Kant, the only satisfaction or fulfillment that matters, if these terms are admissible in Kant's philosophy, is the satisfaction of reason's self-determination, the free and autonomous obedience of the exigencies of pure reason.

III.3e
Kantian Freedom

Accordingly, in Kant freedom has an entirely different meaning from the classical (Greek) meaning. For the ancients, freedom coincides with happiness, since happiness is the life pursued for its own sake. For them, it also coincides with virtue, since the person who has reached self-integration is most deliberate, most in control and at peace, most able to cultivate and follow reason. For Kant, on the other hand, happiness is always suspect (at best) in the moral life, since happiness for him is the heading under which all empirical motives and inclinations fall.[68] To Kant, an ethics based on happiness would be reminiscent of Hobbes, since the pursuit of happiness is always self-interested as concerned with the satisfaction of the empirical self. Therefore, the freedom to pursue happiness so defined can be only license for satisfying individual inclinations, and never the drive towards moral virtue understood as the (Kantian) autonomy of practical reason.

In stark contrast, the ancients see acting virtuously as inherently beneficial for the soul, since you become virtuous by acting virtuously, and being virtuous is being happy (unified and whole). Enjoying virtue, for the ancients, is a sign of moral accomplishment, since the practice of virtue inevitably leads to the formation of the habit of virtue, and habits include pleasure. In this sense, one cannot pursue moral virtue without also pursuing happiness; the two are inseparable.

Kant, however, does not understand freedom in terms of final causality—in terms of the life or activity sought for its own sake—but rather in terms of a self-determined maxim or law that dictates *how* to act universally, but not why, except in general terms. Rational agents should follow the moral law because their autonomous reason binds them (freely) to universality, which is the highest authority for a rational agent. In other words, rational agents should follow the moral law because they are inherently duty-bound to this law. Morality is purely the agent's self-elicited (and

---

68. *Grounding for the Metaphysics of Morals*, First Section, section 405.

therefore free) obedience of the universal law, the coincidence of efficient causality (action) and modern formal causality (law). For the ancients, on the other hand, who also recognized the universality of reason, the purpose of virtue is more concrete: cultivating virtue is cultivating happiness, for the soul and the community, and being happy is being free, since happiness is that for the sake of which everything is done.[69]

In Kant's definition of freedom in terms of law or maxim, one sees the implications of the loss of final causality in the sphere of ethics. In no sense does Kant understand morality as the purpose and fulfillment of the human being as a whole, but rather only as the fulfillment of an elusive and confined aspect—pure reason. This means that Kant's philosophy engages and tries to fulfill only a specialized and fragmented aspect of the human being.

Moral fulfillment lies in autonomy understood as self-elicited and self-imposed law, to be then imposed on the rest of human experience. This law does not grow out of human nature in its purposive orientation, but rather stems from a field outside of nature. In other words, what Kant tries to do in the field of morality is what his predecessor Newton does in the field of physics—the determination of action and interaction through law. Even though Kant's law is free, in being autonomous, while Newton's laws are necessary, both exclude final causality. Both modes of law focus on the formula governing the cases. The difference is that Kant's law governs what should happen, while Newton's law governs what does happen. With Kant, therefore, we see clearly the specialized nature of philosophy against the background of natural science, insofar as Kant's aim is the liberation of rational autonomy through its extraction from the world of nature, from the world of concrete life and experience.[70]

III.3f
Kant's Philosophical Desire

In this specialized project, the impulse and drive behind philosophy are rooted in a fragment of the human being, and philosophy aims accordingly at its particular fulfillment, regardless of the inclinations of the empirical self. Philosophical desire in Kant can only mean reason's love of autonomy.

69. Describing his pursuit of virtue, Socrates famously tells the Athenians, "I make you be happy" (*Apology* 36e).

70. See *Grounding for the Metaphysics of Morals*, Preface, section 389.

In speculative philosophy, this is reason's desire to encounter the scope, limits, and cognitive possibilities of its own inherent structure. In practical philosophy, this is reason's recognition, respect, and will to abide by its own universal standard.

With Kant, as with the other modern philosophers treated in this chapter, philosophy is no longer based on the human being as a whole. However, Kant's own type of fragmentation and specialization will lead to future forms of fragmentation and specialization. Kant is a seminal thinker, and several of his successors take the division between the noumenal and empirical realms seriously, to the extent that they branch out into those who emphasize one of these realms at the expense of the other. For example, one of the current, commonplace divisions of philosophy in terms of the analytic versus the continental tradition may be traced back (to some extent) to Kant's own division.[71]

However, comments on the predicament of philosophical desire today must be reserved for the Conclusion. For now, a few words on Kant's successor and critic, Hegel, will be helpful in seeing the final stage in the development of modern philosophical desire.[72]

III.4
HEGEL'S NEW PHILOSOPHICAL WISDOM

Kant's analysis of a priori knowledge (especially the synthetic one) does help him overcome the skeptical empiricism of Hume. He shows that the mind recognizes, a priori, necessary connections not only analytically but also (and more importantly) synthetically. The mind is therefore autonomous, to the extent that a priori knowledge is not reducible to sense experience. However, Kant's autonomy, as noted, is not a return to Descartes, since Kant recognizes that what the mind contributes to experience is fundamentally regulative or formal, not positive. The mind does not have access to any *being(s)* beyond all possible experience. The mind organizes the contents of experience but does not provide additional content; it does not reach out to things that are outside experience.

71. This is true to the extent that the analytic tradition favors formal and logical analysis, while the continental tradition explores experience and the history of philosophy.

72. In terms of the modern philosophical tendencies initiated by Descartes, and in terms of this book's selection, Hegel represents the final stage. Nietzsche, treated below, breaks away from this modern development.

For the same reasons that Kant overcomes some of the difficulties of Hume's philosophy, Kant also introduces a difficulty of his own that is perhaps even greater. For Kant's position is that experience is the only source for the knowledge of reality, but that this source is known according to the structure of the mind itself. Even though Kant distinguishes between what the mind receives from experience and what the mind contributes to experience, there is no way to know things in themselves, that is, independently of how they appear to the mind, since the mind is the only organ of knowledge.

Descartes' grounding of philosophy in the subject, which ushers in modern philosophy, has developed into subjectivity in Kant. This subjectivity is not individual and empirical, like the subjectivity of Hume and Hobbes, for whom knowledge depends on individual sense perceptions. Rather, Kant's subjectivity is based on the structure of the mind itself. The Copernican revolution reaches philosophy, not with Descartes, but with Kant: just as the heliocentric theory reinterprets the center of the universe, Kant's philosophy reinterprets the center of knowledge. Descartes changes the center of philosophy in terms of philosophical activity, since philosophy now takes place within the subject. However, Kant changes the center of philosophy in terms of knowledge itself, since now the very structure of the knowing subject conditions the form and scope of knowledge.

III.4a
Hegel's Critique of Kant

In Kant's framework, knowledge no longer can be a matter of simply capturing what is objective, what exists extramentally. For knowledge has as much to do with extramental reality as it has to do with the structure of the mind. To what extent does knowledge depend on each of these two factors? All one can say is that things outside the mind constitute the raw material for knowledge, while the mind determines how this raw material is interpreted. Again, since the mind is the sole organ of knowledge, determining the objective status of things in themselves becomes a seemingly impossible task.

This is the core of the critique by G. W. F. Hegel (1770–1831) against Kant: a philosophy based on the conception that knowledge is the relationship between two distinct, separate factors—an organ (the mind) and an object (things in themselves)—is doomed from the start. For there is no possible way to bridge the separation between the organ and the object, so as to gain knowledge of the object in itself, insofar as the object is only accessible through the organ. The organ always stands in the way of the object, since the organ is the medium by which the object is known. Accordingly, one can never distinguish adequately what the organ contributes to the knowledge from what the object in itself contributes, except in very general terms (which say that the mind is the interpreter while objects are the raw material). For Hegel, therefore, Kant's transcendental philosophy, focused on distinguishing the ways in which the mind itself operates as a cognitive organ, actually stands in the way of science, since it does not, and cannot, penetrate reality itself.[73] For Hegel, the possibility for the development of philosophical science must rest on different foundations.

III.4b
Hegel's Modern System

While criticizing Kant's separation between knower and known, Hegel also praises the ancient conception of knowledge, which sees a basic affinity between them.[74] Hegel himself, however, understands and develops this basic affinity, not as Aristotle and Plato did, but in his own way, which falls in line with the general direction of modern philosophy. In this regard, the influence of Spinoza (1632–1677) and his (pantheistic) view that reality is constituted by one substance only, albeit in different modes, is significant.[75] Since knower and known are grounded ultimately in the same reality, the goal for Hegel is unfolding explicitly the consciousness of this knowledge of reality, which is at the same time a self-knowledge. History is also an important part of Hegel's philosophy, and in this sense he may be associated with premodern rather than with modern predecessors (who reject tradition, like Descartes, Hobbes, and Kant). However, again, Hegel's conception of history is found within an overall modern vision.

---

73. See Hegel, *Phenomenology*, Introduction, sections 73–76.

74. See Hegel, *Hegel's Science of Logic*, Introduction, 45.

75. Assessing the sources and definitive import of Hegel's philosophy is a complicated task. Here we mention briefly only basic elements that bear upon the present topic. What is clear is Hegel's intention to supersede Kant's framework by establishing a more solid metaphysical basis for knowledge and science. For an overview of Hegel's philosophy, see Redding, "Georg Wilhelm Friedrich Hegel."

As noted, modern philosophy rests on the rejection of classical thought, to the extent that modern philosophy, beginning with Descartes, is a series of attempts to bridge the gap between the mind and the outside world. To Hegel, however, the beginning of philosophy rests, not on some irreducible separation between knower and known, but on the fundamental relation between them. This relation is presupposed by any distinction between knower and known and is the basis for any assessment of adequacy between knower and known. Hegel's project, therefore, does not aim ultimately at connecting the knower with the known, since this connection is prior to any distinction between them.

For Hegel, the mind or consciousness always holds together the two sides of the relation of knowledge, since consciousness is this relation. Moreover, consciousness also interprets itself in this relation, namely, the adequacy of its own knowledge. For consciousness can either identify or distinguish the knower and the known. Consciousness identifies them when it claims knowledge for itself, while it distinguishes them when it questions its own knowledge, namely, the correspondence between knower and known. This questioning can lead consciousness to revise its own knowledge and reach a more advanced cognitive stage. This latter stage can lead to a higher one, and so on.[76]

In terms of his conception of knowledge, Hegel is no longer working according to the original modern framework. However, Hegel is still a modern, since his work is meant as the solution to the modern problem of knowledge. His aim is the full reconciliation between knower and known. The basic connection between knower and known, by itself, does not constitute the highest grade of knowledge, but only the condition for any knowledge. What in other moderns constitutes the aim, namely, bonding knower and known, in Hegel serves simply as philosophy's precondition. The actual work of philosophy consists in the systematic exposition of the development of knowledge, from its most basic to its final form—what Hegel calls absolute knowing. This exposition, found in the *Phenomenology of Spirit*, traces the cognitive experience of consciousness as it moves from lower to higher stages of knowledge. Hegel also applies this understanding to history. Historical processes mark the development and unfolding of the consciousness of the human spirit.[77]

76. See Hegel, *Phenomenology*, Introduction, sections 77–89.

77. As is well known, Karl Marx adopts Hegelian ideas within a new materialist framework, whereby historical processes culminate in his version of communism.

The exposition of the cognitive experience and development of consciousness is also, in a fundamental sense, a self-exposition, since it is done by consciousness. Accordingly, Hegel's aim is the knowing of knowing, in two chief senses. On the one hand, it is knowledge of the systematic progression of all knowing. On the other hand, and in terms of its ultimate fruition, the aim is self-knowing. Absolute knowing is the point at which consciousness becomes totally reconciled with itself, the point at which the full identity between knower and known is accomplished, and, thereby, all distinction between them is abolished. For Hegel, in other words, all transcendence and all distinction between knower and known must give way to a final identity, to a self-identity, since consciousness is the original fabric that ties together all distinctions, even as it posits them.[78]

III.4c
Hegel and Modern Philosophical Desire

In more than one respect, Hegel's work is the culmination of the chief tendencies of modern philosophy. His work is driven by the mind's desire for rational autonomy and self-knowledge, on the one hand, and by the mind's desire to determine reality, on the other. In Hegel, these drives are reconciled in a system of truth grounded in the very being of consciousness. For these reasons, even though he presupposes a basic affinity rather than a basic gap between knower and known, Hegel is still fundamentally modern. His philosophy is both the product and fulfillment of reason itself, and as such there is no ultimate transcendence in Hegel's system, unlike ancient and medieval philosophy, where love of wisdom is understood as the soul's desire for a divine principle that exceeds the soul.

Moreover, even though Hegel recognizes a wide scope in the experience of consciousness, this experience is treated as equivalent to cognitive process, and this process aims at the mind's undivided self-cognition. The aim of his philosophy is reason's absolute self-knowledge, namely, the knowing of knowing. Even though Hegel's philosophy understands itself as the systematic exposition of the totality of being and knowledge, this philosophy only considers the various dimensions of existence insofar as they contribute to the system, insofar as they embody the sections of a self-contained system of scientific thought. In other words, in serving reason's

---

78. See Hegel, *Phenomenology*, Introduction, section 89.

desire for unmediated self-possession, for systematic and absolute self-knowledge, Hegel's philosophy is still specialized.

In rejecting the basic framework of ancient and medieval philosophy, and in becoming specialized, modern philosophy also rejects the traditional understanding of philosophy as love of wisdom, the understanding that human beings can be only lovers but not possessors of wisdom. From the beginning of modern philosophy, the aim has been some form of capturing what is objective, some form of possession and imposition by the mind.[79] With Hegel's redefined methodology, this modern impulse reaches unmediated fulfillment. With Hegel, therefore, (modern) philosophy becomes through and through the systematic possession of wisdom, but of wisdom understood as the science of reason.

III.5
NIETZSCHE'S AFFIRMATION OF LIFE AND POWER

Modern philosophy, from Descartes to Hegel, is characterized by its emphasis on the problem of knowledge, conceived in terms of the relation between subject and object. Within this framework, this period stresses reason's desire and search for cognition. However, this modern concern with the rational is not exclusive. For example, Blaise Pascal (1623–1662), an accomplished mathematician and contemporary of Descartes, criticizes Descartes' own rational approach to God and explores the alternative of faith. Hobbes himself emphasizes the supremacy of the passions (which include desires and emotions), even though he still accords the issue of cognition basic importance. In addition, there is also a strong strand in modern philosophy that values knowledge in terms of the control of nature, in terms of technological and material advancement. In these ways, at least, modern philosophy also concerns itself with other human dimensions aside from pure reason.

In the case of Friedrich Nietzsche (1844–1900), one finds a sharp rejection of previous philosophy, particularly its rationalist versions. This is not uncommon among thinkers after Hegel, who felt that (modern) philosophy's sharp focus on cognition neglected fundamental features of concrete life and existence. Kierkegaard (1813–1855) criticized the lack of transcendence in Hegel's system and emphasized the existential dimensions of faith,

---

79. In this regard, Hume's praise of the skeptical tradition as healthy and virtuous may be seen as an exception. See *Enquiry*, Section V, Part I, 25–27.

even as he employed dialectical methods akin to those of Hegel. Marx (1818–1883), also influenced by Hegel, and Freud (1856–1939) pointed to economics and sexuality, respectively, as determinative dimensions of human existence. Marx and Freud saw fundamental drives in the human being aside from pure reason, which they analyzed, not like the ancients did, but through their own assumptions and methodologies.

It is noteworthy that after modern philosophy's primary (but not exclusive) interest in the rational, which culminates in Hegel, subsequent philosophers oscillated back to other aspects of the self as their foundation. However, whereas the ancients and medievals recognized the importance of these sources in terms of their contribution to the integration and unity of the soul, these later thinkers developed these sources in terms of their dominance, highlighting the supremacy of the given aspect that they saw as primordial at the expense of other aspects. These later developments are still specialized and fragmented, since they tend to isolate these sources of the self rather than unite them.[80] In the case of Nietzsche, the rejection of rationalism is, concomitantly, the affirmation of a separate, ruling impulse—the desire for power.

III.5a
Nietzsche's Scholarship

A basic feature of Nietzsche's work indicates that he is no longer working within the framework of mainstream modern philosophy. Nietzsche is a philosopher who is equally a scholar, a classical philologist and genealogist. His major modern predecessors rejected the medieval model, whereby philosophical activity is fundamentally the commentary, interpretation, and development of textual sources, with the aim of synthesizing reason and faith. Even though Descartes, Hobbes, and Kant develop very different perspectives, and even though each of them relies to some extent on predecessors, they all seek to establish the foundations of philosophy within the subject. To them, philosophies built upon previous ideas and terms contaminate rather than advance the pursuit of truth by obscuring the subject's own natural judgment, which to them is the only reliable source of truth. By contrast, although his philosophy is by no means a return to the medieval model, Nietzsche derives some of his fundamental positions

---

80. In the modern period, Kant's careful separation of the rational and the empirical is perhaps the most developed expression of this isolation.

from the interpretation of ancient texts. In Nietzsche, the philosopher and the scholar are one.

Nietzsche's own approach to scholarship is another distinguishing feature of his work. To Nietzsche, scholarship, insofar as it considers the expression of cultures through documents and art, considers expressions of life. The goal of the scholar is to understand life as it actually reveals itself in history. Naturally, achieving this goal requires, aside from hermeneutic skill, metaphysical acuity. However, absolute objectivity is impossible, since every point of view is, to some extent, conditioned by the flow of life itself. Moreover, one's own particular perspective could be a mask for deeper, more fundamental motives and tendencies.

With Nietzsche, philosophy becomes humanism, understood as the investigation of the basic tendencies of human life, which by definition questions all previous evaluative criteria. Moreover, this investigation is itself an expression of life. Nietzsche explicitly includes his own philosophical drive within his philosophical aim. To him, there is no such thing as disinterested truth, since seeking truth is part of the will of life, and this will of life is the truth with which the philosopher, the scholar, and the artist should come to terms. Not surprisingly, in Nietzsche's project, there is a transformation of the very notions of truth, life, will, virtue, philosophy, etc. However, as will be shown below, Nietzsche's fundamental insights indicate realities that already have been treated in previous philosophy, though perhaps not in his way.

In one sense, therefore, Nietzsche has brought back the understanding that philosophy should be expressive of the basic yearnings of human nature, since to him genuine philosophy comes to terms with the will of life. On the other hand, Nietzsche did not return to the ancient (or medieval) understanding of the significance of philosophy. To Nietzsche, philosophy is one of life's many expressions, and he certainly sees traditional philosophy as inferior to the more powerful expressions found in certain modes of action and art. Whereas several of his predecessors tried to exclude human nature from the realm of reason, Nietzsche embraces nature and life as the genuine sources of truth. In so doing, however, Nietzsche does not return to the ancient and medieval conception of human nature as a distinct and specific form within the broader realm of natural life. Rather, he understands human life as governed by virtually the same forces governing all life. This position, and its implications, appears with particular clarity in his analysis of virtue and morality.

III.5b
Morality and the Will of Life

Through philological analysis of various languages, Nietzsche discovers what he considers to be the original meanings of good and bad, as well as the transformation of these meanings in history. The first aim of his analysis, based on empirical (textual) and historical evidence, is descriptive, not prescriptive. Through the disclosure of the actual meanings and usages of good and bad as they develop historically, the analysis reveals what these meanings are (and have been), rather than what they should be (or should have been).

In this regard, his approach to morality is the opposite of Kant's, who excludes empirical reality from morals and instead focuses on what universally should be, as determined a priori by reason. Nietzsche's approach also differs from that of the ancients treated in this book, who synthesize the empirical and the ideal through an understanding of human function and purpose.[81] Rather, Nietzsche grounds his morals on empirical evidence, insofar as his chief concern is the historical origin and development of moral concepts. At the same time, however, Nietzsche does end up endorsing some moral concepts over others, to the extent that he finds that they are more genuine—more vital (and therefore truer) expressions of life itself. This preference is a choice among his empirical findings, a judgment of the empirical data that is not provided by the mere data. In favoring some historical manifestations of morality over others, Nietzsche does go beyond mere description and, in so doing, reveals his own philosophical standards and premises.

Nietzsche's fundamental insight in *The Genealogy of Morals* is that originally individuals were considered good and noble on account of their strength and power.[82] Virility, victory, self-affirming action and dominance—these constituted originally the primary sense of the term *good* in reference to human beings. The good were the rulers, the distinguished

---

81. To Plato and Aristotle, the soul thrives in virtue, just as the body thrives in health, since virtue is for the soul the best condition—the purpose and fulfillment—as health is for the body. Even though virtue is the ideal, this ideal is not separate from empirical reality, since even vicious souls are meant for virtue, just as even diseased bodies are meant for health. For virtue and health are the best states and highest modes of fulfillment for soul and body, respectively. The ideal is not only the goal but also a governing principle of empirical reality—souls function relatively well or badly, and are relatively fulfilled, to the extent that they approach complete virtue.

82. *The Genealogy of Morals*, First Essay, section IV.

few, rather than the ruled, the many. In its origin, the basic meaning of the term *good* was closer to the meaning it now possesses when we apply it to, say, boxers and fighting cocks: the good boxer or fighting cock is the one who wins, the one who beats the opponent through his own strength and valor. However, now the term is more generally associated with other traits, such as kindness and generosity, while the original sense of the term only resonates in less common usages.

A vital truth and ontological health stood behind this first expression of goodness. This goodness represented the spontaneous and free expression of the force of life, which, in erecting and expanding its own power, is also invasive, subjugating of what cannot withstand its force—the weaker. The powerful see, feel, and understand their own goodness—their own supremacy—firsthand, in their very being. This sense of goodness stems from the core of the good themselves, from the vital power of life itself. This perspective is genuine because it palpates its own truth, the active, expansive force of its own dominating being—the truest being insofar as it is overwhelming, determinative. In other words, this conception of goodness is voiced by life itself.

The correlative moral concept, that of the bad, is also voiced by life itself. The good, in experiencing their own goodness, distinguish themselves from those whom they dominate—the bad or weak. The good look down upon the bad as their inferiors, despising rather than hating them, since they are not their equals. For the good, the bad are the unfortunate ones who do not have the strength to be active and expansive, but who must rather undergo and be imposed upon. From this biological point of view, weakness is bad insofar as undergoing, yielding, suffering are by definition less vital than the active forces that dominate and order. Strength embodies full-fledged expansion, while weakness is abortive, degenerate, deformed.

However, this original moral perspective, genuine as grounded in life itself, and prevalent in many ancient cultures, is no longer the norm. What is the reason for the decline of aristocratic morality, the morality of the strong, of the few? For Nietzsche, current morality, namely Judeo-Christian morality, which praises charity, suffering, personal sacrifice, and altruism, is a construction of the weak, who artfully and hypocritically reversed the original morality to suit themselves, to gain for themselves the power that they envied in the strong. For Nietzsche, all life, from its most vital to its most degenerate forms, desires power and domination. The difference is that whereas the strong acquire power through free and spontaneous self-expression, through the genuine and healthful manifestation of their own being, the weak, precisely because of their weakness, must resort to deceitful paths.

The weak, by definition, cannot acquire power through the free expression of their own being. Rather, they must lie, pretend, plot, intrigue, and wait for their opportunity. They must use those abilities that they have cultivated through their submission, a condition that they internally resent and hate along with their oppressors but that demands of them outward conformity and obedience. Since the weak's desire for power is saturated with hatred, their object is not only power but also revenge. This hatred, since it must contain itself, since it is too weak to act immediately, festers like a poison, but it festers creatively as it schemes its eventual revenge. For Nietzsche, the greatest fruit—the ultimate revenge—of this creative hatred is the reversal of morality elaborated by the weak, through which they have managed to gain dominance. The most eloquent symbol of their success is the church's seat in Rome, which in classical times was the bastion of the original morality.

The essence of this success lies in the ability to pass weakness off as virtue. Unlike the strong, who see themselves as good and their inferiors as bad, the weak generate a different moral distinction. To the weak, the strong appear evil (not merely bad), since they oppress them and inflict suffering. This perspective on evil, this resentful experience of powerlessness, is the biological source of the morality created by the weak. For by judging the strong as evil, the weak also distinguish themselves from them, and call themselves good by contrast, by default. In this moral valuation, as well as in the moral valuation created by the strong, the strong's expression of power is the original source. The difference is that, in the first case, the strong experienced themselves as good and called themselves good, while in the second case the weak experienced the strong as evil—as their oppressors—and called themselves good by negation, by being not-evil. In other words, the goodness of the weak is not genuine goodness, since it is not experienced as goodness, as a happy and fulfilling condition. On the contrary, the goodness of the weak is suffering, misery, hatred, and desire for revenge. The genius of the weak consists in using this false goodness creatively, to reach what they really value as good, namely, power.[83]

To Nietzsche, the weak have already inherited the earth, to the extent that they have been able to sell their version of morality, to the extent that

83. Ibid., sections X, XV.

now Judeo-Christian (or slave) morality is the dominant morality. By convincingly identifying the traits of weakness with moral worth, such as suffering, sacrifice, and patience, and by disseminating the values that benefit the weak, such as charity and altruism, the weak not only have protected themselves. They also have promoted themselves as most worthy to lead. The advent of modern democracy, socialism, and other forms of mass rule also points to the success of the weak, the many. The weak have gained dominance, not through the expression of any inherent force, since their essence is weakness, but by redefining the value of strength and power, which revaluation also masks their own striving for power.

According to Nietzsche, the merit that the weak claim for themselves in virtue of their weakness is the core of the lie. For the essence of life is its expression. Strength, by definition, manifests itself as strength, since strength is the expansive force that erects itself and overwhelms. Weakness, on the other hand, has no choice but to undergo, to suffer, to yield. Weakness, by definition, submits. Hence, there is no merit in weakness, since there is no choice. If weakness, as weakness, could overwhelm, it would; but then, it would not be weakness, but rather strength. The false idea that the essence of being is hidden and internal, rather than active and expressive, is a metaphysical concomitant of this new, usurping morality. The weak do not assume weakness by choice but by essence, and the strong are not at fault for expressing their strength, since this expression is not by choice but by essence.[84]

Nietzsche's view is that life is what life expresses, that action and deed are the essence of being. Accordingly, the second, newer morality is not a genuine expression of life, but rather a subversion of life, which chokes the vitality of free activity by advocating suffering in this life for the sake of some posited afterlife. Yet, the fundamental motive of this slave morality, and of all expressions of life, however degenerate, is power in this life. This power has been gotten parasitically, by constructing a false morality that undermines strength as it feeds the weak.

In current times, the aristocratic and slave moralities and their tension are part of our inherited moral consciousness. Even though the latter morality has gained ascendancy, the former is still capable of manifesting itself. The old struggle between Rome and Jerusalem is still alive today at the level of moral values.[85]

84. Ibid., section XIII.
85. Ibid., section XVI.

✑

As already indicated, Nietzsche's scholarship not only describes morality's transformation. It also prescribes. According to its own biological standard, it judges the original morality as more genuine, as a truer expression of life than the second form of morality, which is a disfigurement of the first. Nietzsche also considers that the original morality is more likely to approximate objectivity, reason, and justice than a morality based on hatred and revenge. The latter morality is bound to its own resentful point of view, to the compensation of its own personal suffering, and is therefore unable to consider the broader sense of justice. On the other hand, after its wave of force has overwhelmed all resistance, strength comes to rest through its own inertia, in the law and order of consolidated power. The strong, as the conquerors and builders of empires, naturally transition into preservers of a common order. Their intent is not personal compensation or revenge, considerations alien to their own supremacy and achievement, but rather unification and consolidation, which demand legislation. Nevertheless, although the strong might in the end be better equipped for justice than the haters, Nietzsche recognizes that justice only flourishes under exceptional conditions, which are incidental to the essential motivation of the will of life, which is attaining, accumulating, and preserving power. As a by-product of power, as defined by those who happen to rule, justice never can be universal or absolute.[86]

III.5c
Nietzsche and Philosophical Desire

Nietzsche identifies a fundamental vital force, namely, the desire for power, as the determinative and creative impulse in human endeavor. This is evident not only in moral and political terms but also in artistic and scientific terms. For all creativity and knowledge is rooted in the will of life, in the will to power. In grounding its different expressions, the life force also

---

86. "To speak of right and wrong per se makes no sense at all. No act of violence, rape, exploitation, destruction, is intrinsically 'unjust,' since life itself is violent, rapacious, exploitative, and destructive and cannot be conceived otherwise. Even more disturbingly, we have to admit that from the biological point of view legal conditions are necessarily exceptional conditions, since they limit the radical life-will bent on power and must finally subserve, as means, life's collective purpose, which is to create greater power constellations." Ibid., Second Essay, section XI, 208.

grounds their destruction, since life destroys as it renews itself. Nietzsche's god is this supreme Will that expresses itself through us, through all life, by creating and destroying.[87] For this reason, in *The Birth of Tragedy* he argues that art, as the imitation of life, is the metaphysical activity *par excellence*,[88] whether art is understood in terms of images (plastic or Apollonian) or in terms of will (musical or Dionysian).[89] Attic tragedy, in particular—a synthesis of lyric and melody, of the Apollonian and the Dionysian— represents a true artistic high point, since it justifies life here and now in the enjoyment, beauty, and insight of the very synthesis of the creative and destructive dimensions of existence. Attic tragedy reflects the healthy pessimism of those early heroic Greeks, who embraced life here and now along with its imminent destruction and justified it actively and creatively.[90]

In contrast to this vital pessimism, the serenity associated with later Greeks and their theoretical philosophy is a sign of decadence. This attitude, crystallized in Socrates and perpetuated throughout the philosophical tradition, pretends to grab hold of life theoretically, from the point of view of the logical spectator. It pretends to justify life through abstract logical explanations. This theoretical stance, which constructs and appeals to a removed realm of reason, is evidence of the desire to escape rather than to live life. For Nietzsche, Socrates is a destroyer of the art, vitality, and wisdom of the earlier Greek pessimism, and his legacy of logic and reason continues to perpetuate the sterile pretense of the theoretical stance.[91] Nietzsche's own work is aimed at uncovering what he considers to be the fundamental root of truth and life, in order to unmask our true selves, and draw genuinely from this source. All activity is ultimately fueled by the will of life, and his philosophy aims at coming to terms with it.[92]

87. *The Birth of Tragedy*, "A Critical Backward Glance," section V.

88. Ibid., "A Critical Backward Glance," section II. See also ibid., "Preface to Richard Wagner." "A Critical Backward Glance" is part of the second edition of *The Birth of Tragedy*, which first appeared in 1886, while the "Preface to Richard Wagner" is part of the first edition, which appeared in 1872. In the later text, Nietzsche reflects on and criticizes his earlier work, but his criticisms mainly concern style; the fundamental ideas are still advocated.

89. *The Birth of Tragedy*, section I.

90. Ibid., "Critical Backward Glance," section I.

91. Ibid. See also *The Birth of Tragedy*, sections XV, XXIV.

92. When reflecting back on *The Birth of Tragedy*, he claims that the chief task of that work continues to be central for him, namely, to view science or "scholarship from the vantage of the artist and art from the vantage of life" ("Critical Backward Glance," section II, 6).

In one sense, Nietzsche is not unique, insofar as all philosophers ground themselves in certain vital sources that demand certain modes of fulfillment. In the case of Nietzsche, the fulfillment sought is not, as the fulfillment sought in Cartesian philosophy, the autonomous knowledge by pure reason. Rather, the attraction and inspiration of Nietzsche's philosophy lies in the expression of a basic, empirical, vital drive, which also leads him to write quite personally and spontaneously. Nietzsche's writings are sometimes deliberately unsystematic. To Nietzsche, philosophy (like all modes of creation) is fundamentally artistic, in the sense that it is expressive of what he identifies as the life force. Naturally, to him, the author also reveals himself or herself in the creative process. However, just as some moral concepts are more vital and genuine than others, some types of philosophical and artistic creation are more vital and genuine than others. They are more genuine and vital to the extent that they come to terms with the will of life. Not surprisingly, Nietzsche is highly critical of most other philosophers, who develop their projects along different lines.

After the forensic development of cognition in modern philosophy, Nietzsche's dramatic spontaneity represents, among philosophical writings, an explosion of the hitherto neglected empirical self, the drunken self-affirmation of concrete life. His aim is disclosing the life force through scholarship, and capturing its significance through philosophy. In Nietzsche, therefore, philosophical desire is equivalent to love of formulating life—life understood as will to power.

III.5d
Nietzsche's Assessment of the Life Force with Reference to the Ancient Understanding[93]

Several points regarding Nietzsche's perspective are in order. First, it is true that Nietzsche sought to bring back philosophy from the separate realm of reason to the fullness of concrete life. In this regard, he rejects the fragmented and specialized status that philosophy had assumed in the modern period and tries to supply philosophy with broader and more fertile vital sources. However, Nietzsche's philosophy still can be characterized as specialized, in at least two senses. Both senses depend on his position that human nature, like all life, thrives above all in power.

93. The ideas from Plato and Aristotle summarized here are developed more fully in chapter 1.

First, clearly philosophy (Nietzschean or otherwise) is not the greatest expression and fulfillment of the human drive for power (power as understood by Nietzsche). In this regard, political action and artistic creation are at least equal, if not superior, to philosophy. For Nietzsche, philosophy is not the (best) cultivation of human nature as such, as was the case in ancient Greek philosophy. Rather, philosophy is a specialized expression of the will of life, rather than the highest, most comprehensive expression. This appears with particular clarity in the dissonance between Nietzsche's own activity and the activity of those whom he praises above all, in the contrast between Nietzsche the philosopher-scholar and the artists and men of action of whom he speaks. Even if seeking the truth is ultimately driven by power, philosophy is not necessarily even the best avenue to reach truth.[94]

Second, this philosophy appears specialized precisely because its explanatory basis is so broad, precisely because Nietzsche conceives of the ground of human desire as the ground of all life, not specifically human life. Nietzsche comes to identify the drive for power as the fundamental metaphysical drive, as the essence of life itself, and consequently he understands human motivation in these terms. He does not approach human motivation and desire in terms that are specifically human, but rather in the general terms of life itself.

There is no question that human endeavors, including philosophy, are grounded in life itself. There is also no question that power is a fundamental aspect of life, including human life. This has been recognized from the very beginning of philosophy. However, this does not mean, necessarily, that power as conceived by Nietzsche is the all-encompassing motivation or even the most significant and determinative one. For perhaps human motivation and desire follow a pattern of life that is specifically human, rather than the generalized pattern advanced by Nietzsche. If this is true, then his philosophy is specialized insofar as he focuses on human life only in generic terms descriptive of all life, and therefore neglects, or at least downplays, those specific distinguishing properties of human life.

---

94. As noted, Nietzsche's work is indeed quite artistic and personal. At the same time, he does regret at one point that he is not artistic enough: "What a pity that I could not tell as a poet what demanded to be told!" (*Birth of Tragedy*, "A Critical Backward Glance," section III, 7). Perhaps the metaphysical insights in *The Birth of Tragedy* ought to have been sung (he intimates here), or at least (he continues) conveyed through philology. In other words, Nietzsche recognizes that philosophy as practiced by him does not necessarily hold the highest rank in coming to terms with the will of life, with what he considers to be the fundamental truth.

Therefore, a brief contrast with Plato and Aristotle might be helpful at this point, not in order to provide a definitive assessment of Nietzsche's philosophy but rather to understand more clearly the vital source and goal of his philosophy.

The very beginning of Plato's major dialogue, the *Republic*, symbolizes the reality of power and the struggle it produces among human beings. Within this very struggle, there are only two mutually exclusive alternatives, victory or defeat—strength or weakness. Quickly, however, Plato introduces a third option that transcends the power struggle and its two alternatives, namely, persuasion. All this appears in the first exchange between Socrates and his first interlocutor, Polemarchus, whose name appropriately means "the one who begins the battle." Even though the tone of this first exchange seems only half-serious, the theme that it introduces is central to the whole *Republic*.

Polemarchus, accompanied by a large group, wants Socrates and his companion Glaucon, who were heading back to Athens after a festival at the Piraeus, to stay and join them. Polemarchus is set on imposing his will, and warns them that they have no choice, since Polemarchus' group is greater and stronger than the two of them. Socrates responds that perhaps Polemarchus and his group could be persuaded to let them go, but Polemarchus answers that persuasion is futile if they refuse to listen. Socrates grants this point, but after Socrates and Glaucon hear about Polemarchus' plans for the rest of the day, they become interested and decide to stay. In other words, Socrates and Glaucon are the ones who listen and are persuaded. Even though Socrates and Glaucon are the weaker party (in terms of numbers) and end up following the will of the stronger party, they do not simply submit to force, but rather change their minds after discussion. Interestingly, the task of persuading members of the stronger party, notably Polemarchus and Thrasymachus (whose name is also appropriate in the context: "bold in battle"), as well as the task of understanding the true meaning of strength and power, are reserved for the rest of the *Republic*.

Not surprisingly, Socrates' interlocutors, in the *Republic* and other works, are often the strong—vigorous, young nobles of ancient Greece, who are inclined to understand virtue and happiness in terms of victory and domination, whether it be through war or argument (which in the democracy becomes a chief avenue to political success, as the sophists understood). At one level, Socrates' goal in these cases is to persuade the powerful, by engaging them in rational discourse, so that they gradually become attuned to the voice of reason, and recognize in themselves a different authority than their impulse to subjugate.

In the *Republic*, the moment that perhaps most dramatically highlights this aspect of Socrates' activity takes place in Book I, near the end of the exchange between Socrates and Thrasymachus. Thrasymachus embodies life's raw will to dominate, in terms of his aggressive manner, his reputation for shamelessness, and the theses he advances—that justice is nothing but the advantage of the stronger, and that injustice is stronger and more profitable than justice. Surprisingly, however, upon recognizing the inconsistency of his own premises, Thrasymachus does something exceptional for his character: he blushes.[95] After Book I, Thrasymachus is quiet, and it is unclear the extent to which his opinions and character are transformed by his argument with Socrates. Moreover, Thrasymachus' thesis continues to be explored, but along different lines, in the following books. However, the argument with Thrasymachus and its culmination in his act of blushing has made at least one fundamental suggestion: the human soul is influenced not only by its drive for power but also by reason and argument.

It is only in Book IV, however, that the fruition of this suggestion takes place. There, as explained in chapter 1, Plato discusses the nature and strength of the soul, in terms of its three basic drives—the appetitive drive for physical satisfaction, the spirited drive for honor, and the rational drive for knowledge. He locates the desire for power and self-affirmation in the spirited part of the soul primarily. Plato recognizes the tremendous weight of this part of the soul, insofar as the spirit is the part that fights for the whole soul and moves the whole soul toward its goals. At the same time, Plato recognizes that the spirit is not necessarily the supreme part of the soul, although it may assume this role if reason and appetite become subordinate to its demands, if the soul controls its appetites and employs its intelligence in order to overpower others, for the sake of self-affirming dominance. Similarly, the appetitive part may rule the soul, if the soul fights and calculates for the sake of pure physical satisfaction.

Plato's fundamental point, however, is that even though the soul may assume a variety of governments in terms of the power relations among reason, spirit, and appetite, genuine excellence, fulfillment, and strength of soul consists in the harmonious unity of its three parts. This unity occurs only when each part actually performs the role for which it is naturally suited. Reason is naturally suited to rule, since only reason can exercise

---

95. *Republic* 350d.

foresight on behalf of the whole soul and know what is best for the whole soul. The spirit is naturally suited to assist reason, since its natural function is to derive honor by enacting the dictates of reason, while the appetites are naturally suited to obey reason and spirit, since they are best fulfilled through their regulation by the higher parts of the soul. On the other hand, when the parts of the soul engage in roles for which they are not naturally suited, the soul necessarily becomes divided, precisely because its parts are not content performing these roles. This internal conflict undermines and weakens the soul.

For Plato, therefore, the full human expression of the vital force (the soul) arises, not in the struggle of power relations, but rather in justice—in the peaceful unity of the rule of reason, which promotes internal harmony as well as harmony with others, individual as well as social justice. This is the core of his position that justice is stronger than injustice, that justice, understood as the unity of the specifically human vital force, is a more full-fledged and vital manifestation of life than dominance and subjugation. Put simply, Plato recognizes the awesome weight of the human desire for power, but understands its ultimate significance—its ultimate strength—in terms of its contribution to a broader unity, to the organization of the human life force in terms that transcend power as understood by Nietzsche. For Plato, as for Nietzsche, the strong, the vital, the virtuous are the aristocratic few. Virtue is difficult and, therefore, praiseworthy. For Plato, however, the true aristocrats are not simply those with the strength to defeat the opposition, but rather those who rule their lives through reason, who are also the ones most fit to rule governments. For Plato, unlike Nietzsche, justice is not an incidental and exceptional by-product of strength. Rather, strength is equivalent to justice, since justice is the fruition of the soul, the vital force. For this reason, for Plato philosophy, rightly understood, is the highest cultivation of the soul, the best path to virtue and happiness, and not merely one among several genuine expressions of the will of life. In pursuing philosophy, Plato, more than Nietzsche, does what he prescribes.

Aristotle also, like Nietzsche and Plato, understands philosophy and all human endeavor as grounded in and expressive of the life force. According to Aristotle, all natural beings seek their highest mode of vitality, namely, the actualization of their potencies. However, closer to Plato than to Nietzsche, he analyzes the life force as specified according to various natural forms. Human life shares generic properties with other living things—nutrition and growth with plants and animals, perception and locomotion with nonrational animals. However, these generic properties, as found in human life, are specified by humanity's distinguishing and determinative feature, by the feature that sets human life apart from other forms of life, namely, reason.

According to Aristotle, the human vital force inherently seeks to strengthen itself, insofar as it inherently desires actualization. Through this inherent aim, power and domination can play very large and even determinative roles in human life. However, the soul that seeks purely to overpower others, and to affirm itself in this domination, is not the most virtuous or strongest soul. The highest, pleasantest, and most vital expression of the human life force consists in actualization through the rule of reason, since reason is meant to be the authoritative element in human life, insofar as reason specifies human life. Accordingly, the most powerful expression of the life force is the development of the intellectual and moral virtues, which order and unify the soul and which, consequently, promote peace and justice. In other words, Aristotle understands the human drive for vital strength in broader terms than simply power, or to put it in another way, he understands genuine human power as something different from self-affirming domination.

For Aristotle (and Plato), philosophy not only helps us discover the best way of life. It is also the best way of life, since the philosophical life best actualizes our potencies. Philosophy leads to the strongest and most developed state of the human life force. For Aristotle, as for Nietzsche and Plato, the strong are the aristocratic few. However, like Plato, and unlike Nietzsche, Aristotle's aristocratic few are the true philosophers. They are few because, again, virtue is difficult. Hence Aristotle, more than Nietzsche, does what he prescribes and admires.

Nietzsche, then, rejects his modern predecessors and brings philosophy back to concrete life, and to a more ancient understanding of reality, insofar as he grounds much of his analysis in the study of ancient texts. In the ancient tradition itself, however, there are other alternatives for a philosophy of life, as one may gather from Plato and Aristotle. In a fundamental sense, these alternatives provide a broader, and perhaps richer, understanding of (human) life, and of philosophy insofar as it reflects and bears upon life. This is not to dismiss Nietzsche's own unique insights. However, these alternatives are important sources for anyone who wishes to reflect seriously on the basic motivations for human activity in general, and philosophical activity in particular.

Conclusion

As outstanding philosophers, the thinkers selected in this study are still relevant today. The attitudes and views of such historical figures are always contemporary, to the extent that readers can find them truthful, worthwhile, or interesting. To validate their relevance, no other justification is necessary aside from the stimulus they can bring to the contemporary reader. This is to identify with them at some level. On the other hand, our lack of affinity with some of them might not be sufficient to disregard them as irrelevant to our lives. Perhaps greater attention or effort is required in order to appreciate them.

This study sought two related things. It sought (1) to make different philosophies accessible to the reader, while (2) capturing their essential desires and goals. Defining the desire characteristic of each philosophy requires a basic analysis of the philosopher's view. Philosophical desire is manifested in the philosophical pursuit, concretely through rational investigation and analysis leading to the aspired goal of truth. Accordingly, this study provides an account of fundamental principles, arguments, and conclusions of the philosophers, sometimes quite in detail. It also presents the philosophers historically and explains how they build on and depart from each other. Accordingly, this work can serve as a historical introduction to philosophy, from Socrates to Nietzsche.

Analyzing major historical figures in light of the theme of philosophical desire introduces philosophy well. After all, at its origin, philosophy defines itself as a type of desire more than anything else, namely, as the love of wisdom, as explained in the Introduction and chapter 1. Accordingly, the unique approach of this work is naturally suited to introduce philosophy to beginners, by making them appreciate the origin of philosophy and by providing a framework against which to assess important changes and transformations in the history of philosophy. The book not only offers an answer to the question, what is philosophy? It also looks at how the very meaning of philosophy undergoes modifications. Thus, through its own approach and lens, this work still has something to offer to the advanced student who is already familiar with the included philosophers but who may not have assessed them in terms of the philosophical desire that they manifest and represent.

It is the author's hope that the work has been useful for the reader, in terms of approaching different views and in terms of reflecting on the nature of philosophical desire, both generally and personally as it relates to the reader's own affinities.

∾

To be sure, our investigation of philosophical desire has been limited by the selection of material. However, it treated major representatives of important currents of philosophical desire, which together give the topic a broad and diverse context. This suffices to draw basic conclusions regarding differences within the spectrum of philosophical desire, as well as regarding the historical transformation of this desire.

Let us now set forth the main conclusions, already evidenced in the body of this work. First, philosophical desire follows different patterns in the ancient, medieval, and modern periods. There is, of course, diversity within each of these periods. However, certain fundamental commonalities underlie each of these periods, at least in terms of the thinkers included in this work. Even though Socrates, Plato, and Aristotle offer different perspectives, the three understand love of wisdom as a desire stemming from the soul as a whole (character and intellect), which accordingly aims at the fulfillment of the whole soul through virtue and knowledge. This is developed in chapter 1, and summarized in section I.4.

In spite of important differences among medieval philosophers, this common core of ancient Greek love of wisdom is adopted by the medievals, by Augustine, Thomas Aquinas, and many others who develop the wisdom of the Greeks. However, Augustine and Aquinas reinterpret classical Greek love of wisdom in light of revelation. Accordingly, they understand the soul and its goal in a new light: made in the image of God, the soul desires union with God. Love of wisdom is ultimately love of the God of revelation. This supernatural goal requires reason, faith, and grace. The medieval lover of wisdom, therefore, is no longer the pure philosopher in the classical sense, but rather the one who synthesizes reason and revelation, natural and supernatural sources of wisdom. There is a common core of ancient and medieval love of wisdom: the desire for fulfillment of the soul as a whole. However, there is a proper core of medieval love of wisdom in terms of reinterpreting and reorienting the ancient Greek understanding in light of faith. This is developed in chapter 2, and summarized in section II.3.

The common fabric of love of wisdom underlying ancient and medieval philosophy is broken in the modern period. Among the modern philosophers of chapter 3, there is no longer love of wisdom understood as all-encompassing desire seeking all-encompassing fulfillment. In terms of philosophical desire, this is the fundamental break in the history of philosophy.

Ancients and medievals understood love of wisdom above all as the pursuit of happiness, which includes moral and intellectual virtue, the perfection of the character and the intellect. To them, love of wisdom aims at making the soul complete by making it excellent and wise. To them, love of wisdom is an essentially human desire, rooted in the core of what it means to be human, and aiming at the proper fulfillment of this core. Love of wisdom is not a specialized desire, divorced from fundamentally human yearnings and exigencies. On the contrary, love of wisdom aims at organizing these yearnings and exigencies in the best way, for the sake of integration, well-being, and completion.

Modern philosophy no longer recognizes, implicitly or explicitly, this common root or core or unifying principle. As a result, philosophy becomes specialized. Instead of being humanly unifying, the desires governing modern philosophical endeavor are specialized or fragmented as rooted in isolated aspects of the self. Descartes, for reasons of his own, grounds philosophy in the subject considered strictly as a thinking thing. In his case, philosophy becomes the desire and fulfillment of the thinking self only, not of the human being as a whole. The other moderns treated in this book ground their philosophies on different dimensions of human existence, but they perpetuate this pattern of fragmentation and specialization. Their efforts reject the very idea of philosophical unity as understood by the ancients and medievals. Instead, they justify their approaches through narrower bases, which nevertheless provide new insights and perspectives, some of which have tremendous and continuing impact.

Considering the broad historical spectrum of philosophical desire, the basic issue is whether one understands it as a unifying or as a specialized desire, as answering a calling of the human being as a whole or as answering a calling of a narrower demand. In terms of the former, this book provides ample material for reflection, a variety of perspectives assessing this unifying human core, its fundamental desire, and the pursuit of its goal. In terms of the latter, this book also provides a variety of perspectives that give powerful reasons justifying these narrower demands and their fruits. Throughout this work, we have reserved the term "love of wisdom" to indicate the former desire, embodied by ancients and medievals. As the subtitle of this book suggests, "philosophical desire" is the broader term that applies to all philosophers in this book, not only to those modern thinkers who embody the latter, narrower desires.

This ancient, medieval, and modern background reveals (to some extent) what philosophy has been and what it has and can become, its origins and possibilities. This philosophical spectrum is useful in thinking about one's own approach to philosophy, about what one aspires to obtain from and through philosophy. This background, which continues to influence thinkers beyond Nietzsche, is basic for additional research and reflection on these key questions.

Perhaps the two basic modes of philosophical desire can and even should coexist in some way. Unifying desire does not exclude by definition specialized desire, or vice versa. Properly understood and balanced, they could even be mutually enriching. Genuine lovers of wisdom have contributed and still can contribute in a variety of theoretical and practical fields. However, the modern trends toward specialization and fragmentation have grown by now beyond anything imaginable in the modern period itself (ending with Nietzsche in terms of our study). Philosophy now almost completely has become philosophies. Its unity is compromised. This is not meant in the sense that there are a variety of philosophical schools and outlooks. This variety always has existed.

As explained in the Introduction, the difference is that now more than ever philosophy has become broken up and dependent. Much of it is defined as absorbed into already specialized fields, as in philosophy of biology, philosophy of literature, etc. Academic philosophers, even those whose work is associated with fundamental areas like metaphysics and ethics, spend careers on the production of narrowly defined research, and nothing else. Institutional and economic practices, agendas, and requirements, ordered towards the production of *new* scholarship, intensify the specification and division of philosophy. In this trend, modern and contemporary philosophers will continue to be important sources for the development and assessment of specific knowledge. Even ancients and medievals can and have been tapped according to what in them may bear upon these specialized areas and concerns.

However, as suggested, this specialization and the important role of philosophy within it do not exclude by definition the contemporary relevance of the ancient and medieval model discussed in this book. On the contrary, this model still has something to offer us, precisely because of the increasing specialization and fragmentation of our day. Is there a unifying core to the human being? If so, what is the highest and best fulfillment according to this core? Is there a fundamental unity underlying all reality? If so, how do we reach the best possible vision according to this unity? It is difficult to see how these questions can have no relevance today. At the heart of our experience lies the sense of unity, the sense that the various dimensions of our humanity somehow fit within an overall totality, the sense that the various dimensions of reality somehow fit within a fundamental order. The ancient and medieval thinkers provide us with some of the richest discussions of these questions, helping us come to terms with what is unifying in our lives.

Are we called to pursue unity—unity of self and unity of vision? This is the first and final question of this book. If we recognize something vital, meaningful, or compelling in this question, it is because we recognize (however obliquely) some unifying core to our desire, which seeks the fulfillment of this core. It is because we recognize (however obliquely) the original meaning of love of wisdom, not merely nominally or conceptually, but wholly, as unifying desire seeking integrated fulfillment.

Ancients and medievals harness this desire towards its goal. As they realized, mortals as such never can be fully wise. They can approach wisdom, but they remain lovers, not possessors, of wisdom. Previous thinkers can be of great help, but they must be assimilated within a deliberate, active, and personal context, that is, within a way of life. Plato relies on Socrates, Aristotle on Plato, etc. However, the great thinkers are neither perfect nor the last word, and they sometimes disagree. It is up to us to gather from them, and from any other relevant source, what is necessary for our pursuit. Ultimately, the work is ours.

Even if we agree with these original philosophers in recognizing love of wisdom as unifying love, we will still express and pursue this desire in our own way, in the fullness and concreteness of our humanity. What is undeniable is that the great ancient and medieval thinkers can help guide us, since they explore the depths of that unifying desire called love of wisdom. They still can be helpful in coming to terms with what is basic and essential in us, with our very selves.

For this reason, love of wisdom in its original sense will always be current, no matter how far we branch out in our specialized interests and concerns. It is within this basic, unifying pursuit, perhaps, that we might best be able to assess the worth of more specialized concerns. Even if the academic discipline of philosophy one day becomes fragmented through and through, as long as human beings continue to yearn for true wholeness, love of wisdom never will.

Bibliography

Aristotle. *De Anima*. Translated by J. A. Smith. In *The Basic Works of Aristotle*, edited by Richard McKeon, 533–603. New York: Modern Library, 2001.

———. *Metaphysics*. Translated by W. D. Ross. In *The Basic Works of Aristotle*, edited by Richard McKeon, 681–926. New York: Modern Library, 2001.

———. *Nicomachean Ethics*. Translated by W. D. Ross. In *The Basic Works of Aristotle*, edited by Richard McKeon, 927–1112. New York: Modern Library, 2001.

———. *Physics*. Translated by R. P. Hardie and R. K. Gaye. In *The Basic Works of Aristotle*, edited by Richard McKeon, 213–394. New York: Modern Library, 2001.

———. *Posterior Analytics*. Translated by G. R. G. Mure. In *The Basic Works of Aristotle*, edited by Richard McKeon, 108–86. New York: Modern Library, 2001.

Aquinas, Thomas. *On Being and Essence*. In *Philosophy in the Middle Ages: The Christian, Islamic, and Jewish Traditions*, edited by Arthur Hyman et al. 3rd ed. Indianapolis: Hackett, 2010.

———. *Summa Theologica*. In *Basic Writings of Saint Thomas Aquinas*. Edited by Anton C. Pegis. 2 vols. Indianapolis: Hackett, 1997.

Augustine. *The City of God*. In *Augustine: Political Writings*, translated by Michael W. Tkacz and Douglas Kries, edited by Ernest L. Fortin and Douglas Kries, 3–201. Indianapolis: Hackett, 1994.

———. *Confessions*. Translated by Henry Chadwick. Oxford: Oxford University Press, 2008.

———. *Eighty-Three Different Questions*. Translated by David L. Mosher. Fathers of the Church 70. Washington, DC: Catholic University of America Press, 2002.

———. *On Free Choice of the Will*. Translated by Thomas Williams. Indianapolis: Hackett, 1993.

———. *The Trinity*. Translated by Edmund Hill. Edited by John Rotelle. Works of Saint Augustine, pt. 1, vol. 5. Brooklyn: New City, 1991.

Bacon, Francis. *De Dignitate et Augmentis Scientiarum*. Works of Francis Bacon 7. London: Paternoster Row, 1824.

Bonaventure. *The Journey of the Mind to God*. Translated by Philotheus Boehner. Edited by Stephen F. Brown. Indianapolis: Hackett, 1993.

Brown, Stephen F., and Juan Carlos Flores. *Historical Dictionary of Medieval Philosophy and Theology*. Historical Dictionaries of Religions, Philosophies and Movements 76. Lanham, MD: Scarecrow, 2007.

Burtt, Edwin A. *The Metaphysical Foundations of Modern Science*. Mineola, NY: Dover, 2003.

Cunningham, Lawrence S., and John J. Reich. *Culture and Values: A Survey of the Humanities*. 7th ed. Boston: Wadsworth, 2009.

Curd, Patricia, ed. *A Presocratics Reader*. Indianapolis: Hackett, 1996.

Descartes, René. *Discourse on Method; and, Meditations on First Philosophy*. Translated by Donald A. Cress. 4th ed. Indianapolis: Hackett, 1998.

Flores, Juan Carlos. *Henry of Ghent: Metaphysics and the Trinity; with a Critical Edition of Question Six of Article Fifty-Five of the* Summa Quaestionum Ordinariarum. Ancient and Medieval Philosophy, Series 1, 36. Leuven: Leuven University Press, 2006.

———. "The Intersection of Philosophy and Theology: Henry of Ghent on the Scope of Metaphysics and the Background in Aquinas and Bonaventure." *Revista Portuguesa de Filosofia* 71 (2015) 531–44.

———. "The Roots of Love of Wisdom: Henry of Ghent on Platonic and Aristotelian Forms." In *Philosophy and Theology in the Long Middle Ages: A Tribute to Stephen F. Brown*, edited by Kent Emery Jr. et al., 623–40. Studien und Texte zur Geistesgeschichte des Mittelalters 105. Leiden: Brill, 2011.

Hadot, Pierre. *Philosophy as a Way of Life: Spiritual Exercises from Socrates to Foucault*. Translated by Michael Chase. Oxford: Blackwell, 1995.

Hegel, G. W. F. *Hegel's Science of Logic*. Translated by A. V. Miller. Amherst, NY: Humanities Press, 1969.

———. *Phenomenology of Spirit*. Translated by A. V. Miller. Oxford: Oxford University Press, 1977.

Hobbes, Thomas. *Leviathan*. Edited by Edwin Curley. Indianapolis: Hackett, 1998.

Hume, David. *Dialogues Concerning Natural Religion*. Edited by Richard H. Popkin. 2nd ed. Indianapolis: Hackett, 1998.

———. *An Enquiry Concerning Human Understanding*. Edited by Eric Steinberg. 2nd ed. Indianapolis: Hackett, 1993.

Kant, Immanuel. *Critique of Pure Reason*. Translated by Werner S. Pluhar. Indianapolis: Hackett, 1996.

———. *Grounding for the Metaphysics of Morals*. Translated by James W. Ellington. 3rd ed. Indianapolis: Hackett, 1993.

———. *Prolegomena to Any Future Metaphysics*. Translated by James W. Ellington. 2nd ed. Indianapolis: Hackett, 2001.

Morgan, Michael L., ed. *Classics of Moral and Political Theory*. 5th ed. Indianapolis: Hackett, 2011.

Nietzsche, Friedrich. *The Birth of Tragedy and The Genealogy of Morals*. Translated by Francis Golffing. Garden City, NY: Doubleday, 1956.

Pieper, Josef. *Leisure, the Basis of Culture; The Philosophical Act*. Translated by Alexander Dru. San Francisco: St. Ignatius, 2009.

Plato. *Apology*. Translated by G. M. A. Grube. In *Complete Works*, edited by John M. Cooper, 17–36. Indianapolis: Hackett, 1997.

———. *Crito*. Translated by G. M. A. Grube. In *Complete Works*, edited by John M. Cooper, 37–48. Indianapolis: Hackett, 1997.

———. *Euthyphro*. Translated by G. M. A. Grube. In *Complete Works*, edited by John M. Cooper, 1–16. Indianapolis: Hackett, 1997.

———. *Five Dialogues*. Translated by G. M. A. Grube. Revised by John M. Cooper. 2nd ed. Indianapolis: Hackett, 2002.

———. *Phaedo*. Translated by G. M. A. Grube. In *Complete Works*, edited by John M. Cooper, 49–100. Indianapolis: Hackett, 1997.

————. *Phaedrus*. Translated by Alexander Nehamas and Paul Woodruff. In *Complete Works*, edited by John M. Cooper, 506–56. Indianapolis: Hackett, 1997.

————. *Protagoras*. Translated by Stanley Lombardo and Karen Bell. In *Complete Works*, edited by John M. Cooper, 746–90. Indianapolis: Hackett, 1997.

————. *Republic*. Translated by G. M. A. Grube; revised by C. D. C. Reeve. In *Complete Works*, edited by John M. Cooper, 971–1223. Indianapolis: Hackett, 1997.

————. *Sophist*. Translated by Nicholas P. White. In *Complete Works*, edited by John M. Cooper, 235–93. Indianapolis: Hackett, 1997.

————. *Symposium*. Translated by Alexander Nehamas and Paul Woodruff. In *Complete Works*, edited by John M. Cooper, 457–505. Indianapolis: Hackett, 1997.

————. *Theaetetus*. Translated by M. J. Levett; revised by Myles Burnyeat. In *Complete Works*, edited by John M. Cooper, 157–234. Indianapolis: Hackett, 1997.

————. *Timaeus*. Translated by Donald J. Zeyl. In *Complete Works*, edited by John M. Cooper, 1224–91. Indianapolis: Hackett, 1997.

Redding, Paul. "Georg Wilhelm Friedrich Hegel." *The Stanford Encyclopedia of Philosophy* (Fall 2015). http://plato.stanford.edu/archives/fall2015/entries/hegel/.

CPSIA information can be obtained
at www.ICGtesting.com
Printed in the USA
LVOW11*2032200318

570507LV00005BA/73/P